COMBAT AIRCRAFT

120 Ju 52/3m BOMBER AND TRANSPORT UNITS 1936-41

SERIES EDITOR TONY HOLMES

120 COMBAT AIRCRAFT

Robert Forsyth

Ju 52/3m BOMBER AND TRANSPORT UNITS 1936–41

OSPREY
PUBLISHING

First published in Great Britain in 2017 by Osprey Publishing
PO Box 883, Oxford, OX1 9PL, UK
1385 Broadway, 5th Floor, New York, NY 10018, USA
E-mail: info@ospreypublishing.com

OSPREY is a trademark of Osprey Publishing, a division of Bloomsbury Publishing Plc

Osprey Publishing, part of Bloomsbury Publishing Plc
© 2017 Osprey Publishing

All rights reserved. Apart from any fair dealing for the purpose of private study, research, criticism or review, as permitted under the Copyright, Design and Patents Act 1988, no part of this publication may be reproduced, stored in a retrieval system, or transmitted in any form or by any means, electronic, electrical, chemical, mechanical, optical, photocopying, recording or otherwise without prior written permission. All enquiries should be addressed to the publisher.

A CIP catalogue record for this book is available from the British Library

ISBN: 978 1 4728 1880 5
PDF e-book ISBN: 978 1 4728 1881 2
ePub ISBN: 978 1 4728 1882 9
XML ISBN: 978 1 4728 2140 9

Edited by Tony Holmes
Cover Artwork by Mark Postlethwaite
Aircraft Profiles by Jim Laurier
Index by Sandra Shotter
Originated by PDQ Digital Media Solutions, UK
Printed in China through World Print Ltd.

17 18 19 20 21   10 9 8 7 6 5 4 3 2 1

Osprey Publishing supports the Woodland Trust, the UK's leading woodland conservation charity. Between 2014 and 2018 our donations will be spent on their Centenary Woods project in the UK.

www.ospreypublishing.com

Front Cover
Following orders issued directly by Adolf Hitler to send aerial attacks against 'installations essential for the maintenance of life' in Warsaw, a *Kette* (three aircraft-element) of Ju 52/3ms from Oberstleutnant Hans Alefeld's IV./KG.z.b.V.2, based at Breslau-Gandau, emerges from the smoke caused by the dropping of incendiary bombs over the city on 25 September 1939. The local Luftwaffe air commander, Generalmajor Wolfram Frhr. von Richthofen, had intended the bombing of Warsaw to be conducted by He 111s, but his request for such aircraft was turned down. Instead, the Ju 52/3m transports of IV./KG.z.b.V.2 were hastily and crudely 'adapted' to perform as makeshift bombers by means of each aircraft carrying two members of the *Geschwader*'s groundcrew who were tasked with the job of shovelling out incendiary bombs from the Junkers' fuselage hatches using spades.
   Many Ju 52/3ms flew at low level over the city and dropped more than 70 tons of incendiaries via such a method. They caused large fires that resulted in a pall of thick black smoke forming over the suburbs. The smoke eventually reached a height of 3500 m as it drifted off towards the southeast.
   On the morning of 27 September the city of Warsaw capitulated, many of its buildings destroyed and thousands of its inhabitants having been killed. IV./KG.z.b.V.2 relocated back to Breslau and was disbanded in November. As far as is known the Luftwaffe never again – officially – deployed the Ju 52/3m as a bomber. Mark Postlethwaite's dramatic painting depicts aircraft of 13. *Staffel*, KG.z.b.V.2 as they prepare to leave the target

Previous Pages
Paratroops remove a trolley of metal storage canisters from a Ju 52/3mge as part of a preparatory training session ahead of operations in the West in May 1940. The aircraft has been fitted with a cockpit MG 15 machine gun on a ring mounting and is adorned with larger than standard underwing crosses

CONTENTS

CHAPTER ONE
WAR AND PEACE 6

CHAPTER TWO
SPANISH SKIES 21

CHAPTER THREE
'WHETHER MEN, FUEL, BOMBS OR BREAD' 52

CHAPTER FOUR
ATTACK IN THE NORTH 59

CHAPTER FIVE
ATTACK IN THE WEST 67

CHAPTER SIX
POWDER KEG 80

APPENDICES 90

COLOUR PLATES COMMENTARY 91
SOURCES AND BIBLIOGRAPHY 94
INDEX 96

CHAPTER ONE

WAR AND PEACE

In October 1920, a quietly spoken 23-year-old former soldier and ship designer by the name of Ernst Zindel joined a small aviation research bureau set up by the respected aircraft designer Professor Hugo Junkers in the Saxony-Anhalt town of Dessau, lying at the junctions of the Mulde and Elbe rivers. Junkers, whose entrepreneurial and academic talents had earned him an impressive reputation within the German aircraft and engineering industries, and Zindel, a Bavarian who had been badly wounded while serving with an infantry regiment in World War 1, would go on to enjoy a close and profitable relationship until Junkers' death in 1935.

Zindel had been attracted by Junkers' insightful and progressive use of metal in the aircraft which he had designed and which had been manufactured by his Junkers Flugzeugwerk company, but he had joined the firm at a difficult time. Despite Junkers' burgeoning manufacturing interests, which included the production of water heaters, metal buildings and furniture, the post-war economic environment and the drastic restrictions of the Treaty of Versailles in Germany cast a dark shadow over the company, forcing him to cut back his workforce from around 2000 employees to just 200. No longer permitted to build aeroplanes – or at least operating with severe curtailment – Junkers Flugzeugwerk placed its emphasis on the production of water heaters, calorimeters, metal furniture, cutlery and household appliances.

Lufthansa's Ju 52/3m Wk-Nr 5294 D-AMAK *VOLKMAR VON ARMIN* parked off the apron at Taliedo aerodrome in Milan. The aircraft bears the national tail markings used prior to the Nazis taking power in Germany

Ernst Zindel (left) joined the Junkers firm in 1920 and quickly became one of Hugo Junkers' key men. From 1927 he was officially the company's chief design engineer, though to all intents and purposes he had filled that role since 1923. A modest and incredibly knowlegeable man, he was involved in the design and development of many of Junkers' aircraft, but arguably the Ju 52/3m was his greatest legacy. He remained with Junkers through to 1945. He is seen here with a model of Ju 52/3mg2e Wk-Nr 5093, coded D-ALUG and named *JOSEF ZAURITZ* by Deutsche Luft Hansa. By spring 1940 this aircraft was serving with KGr.z.b.V.106. On the table in front of Zindel are scale drawings of the Ju 52/3m

Initially, metalwork for all Junkers' products had been undertaken by hand using the traditional skills of tinsmiths and blacksmiths, but in the case of the aeroplane construction that remained, the firm had introduced Duralumin. It was not all plain sailing. Considerable investigative work had been needed to overcome the unavoidable problems of corrosion and fatigue, as well to devise improvements in joining, welding and riveting. Of particular concern was the problem of corrosion inside tubing and frameworks.

Eventually, however, after persevering with sheet metal, it was recognised that corrugated Duralumin was a very suitable material. Although the parasitic drag associated with corrugated Duralumin was more of a problem than with smooth skins, it was not too much of an issue when considering the relatively low aircraft speeds of the time. Joining corrugated metal panels or joining them to smooth panels, however, were difficult processes requiring considerable skill. Nevertheless, during the post-war years, Junkers did introduce a number of greatly valued machines and machine processes that were subsequently widely adopted in aeronautical metal engineering, such as stretching, swaging (forged reduction), upsetting (forged increasing), turning, stamping and pressing.

Finally, the ban on the manufacture of commercial aircraft in Germany was lifted in 1922 as a result of 'definition of use' and Junkers resumed work in construction, the testing of materials and wind tunnel testing. However, an ill-fated venture with the Russian government during the early 1920s had almost resulted in financial disaster. Germany had been eager to cooperate in any bi-lateral ventures with Russia to allow continued – if not covert – development of its aircraft industry. By signing the Treaty of Rapello, Russia had declared herself willing to place airfields, aircraft manufacturing facilities and labour at Germany's disposal in return for German technical knowledge and training. The potential for the mass manufacture of aircraft in Russia, free of Allied intervention was irresistible.

In November 1922, encouraged by the German government to the tune of 100 million Reichsmarks, Junkers signed a contract with the Russian government to build airframes and engines designed by his company for use by the Soviet Air Force at a factory near Moscow. Professor Junkers was well aware that a lucrative market still existed for military aircraft as well as civil, and that wherever possible every commercial type should be built with potential military conversion in mind.

Meanwhile, Junkers went at full pelt to build a series of all-metal aircraft, including the single-engined F 13, the world's first metal airliner, the origins of which went back to 1919. Such was the ensuing success and reliability of the F 13 that, by the late 1920s, examples were in service in more than 30 countries including the USA, Bolivia, Colombia, Austria, Great Britain, Italy, Persia, Poland, Russia, Denmark, Estonia, Finland, Latvia, Sweden and Switzerland.

In 1923 work was completed on the A 20, a mass-produced, purpose-built, low-wing mail and aerial mapping monoplane, again made of Duralumin and powered by either a 160 hp Mercedes D IIIa engine in the case of those aircraft manufactured by Junkers, or by a 220 hp

Junkers L 2 in the case of aircraft built by the Swedish-based Junkers subsidiary, AB Flygindustri. The A 20 was operated by the Junkers-Luftverkehr airline on its overnight mail service between Warnemünde and Karlshamm, in Sweden, while a new German airline, Luft Hansa, used at least ten aircraft for the carriage of night mail, newspapers and general freight. Other users included Swiss, Chinese and Chilean carriers and the Turkish military air arm. A small quantity was also built in Russia for the Soviet Air Force.

Between 1924 and 1928, Junkers produced several successful, if short-lived, commercial designs, including the J 23 (G 23), the firm's first three-engined machine. The J 23 would be the forerunner of many successive multi-engined, all-metal, cantilever transport aircraft and was essentially an enlarged F 13, the production of which was prompted as a result of demand from the steadily burgeoning German air transport market. While an outstanding aeroplane for its size, the F 13 could carry only four to five passengers and limited freight, whereas the new design called for accommodation for up to nine passengers. At first the J 23 suffered from limitations in power imposed by the Versailles restrictions, which stipulated that only two 100 hp Mercedes and one Junkers L 2 engine could be fitted. The latter was a four-stroke, six-cylinder, in-line petrol engine built by the Junkers' engine business, Junkers Motorenbau.

The J 23/G 23 was thus considerably under powered. This situation was rectified in 1925 when later variants were fitted with Mercedes D IIIas and uprated Junkers L 2s. Production of the G 23 was modest, however, with some aircraft being built in Sweden. A small number were, nevertheless, sold to Swedish and Swiss airlines.

Originally designed as a single-engine aircraft, the G 24 evolved from the G 23, of which there was a production run of 60 machines. The G 24 featured a larger airframe, in which a crew of three and nine passengers could be accommodated, with the crew enjoying semi-closed or entirely covered cockpits. It was powered by three Junkers 195 hp L 2 or 310 hp L 5 engines. The G 24 won international recognition in 1926 when two examples made a 20-stage, long-range, route-proving flight from Berlin, across Siberia, to the Far East. Landing at Peking on 30 August, the two aircraft returned to Berlin in late September, having flown for 140 hours. Then, in 1927, a G 24 was airborne for more than seven hours, carrying a payload of 2000 kg for 1013 km, while a few days later, another flew for more than 14 hours carrying a load of 1000 kg for just over 2000 km. In June the type attained a speed of 207.26 km/h carrying a payload of 2000 kg for over 100 km.

These were record-breaking accomplishments that went hand in hand with increased comfort for passengers in the form of leather armchairs, overhead luggage nets, toilets, flight attendants and complimentary route maps. Even typewriters and radio telephones were available for business travellers.

By 1926, despite the shackles of the Versailles Treaty, Germany was viewed by many as the most 'air-minded' nation in Europe. But for Junkers, the venture into Russia had not worked out. The firm had apparently used subsidies granted for manufacture in Russia to cover the cost of

As a result of restrictions imposed on Germany by the Treaty of Versailles, Hugo Junkers was forced to suspend work on the manufacture of metal aircraft during the 1920s and instead placed emphasis on the production of domestic appliances such as water heaters (an example of which is seen here), metal furniture and cutlery

The three L 2 engines of a Junkers G 24 run up as it prepares to taxi out in 1929. One of several, state-of-the-art, all-metal Junkers designs, the G 24 proved itself as a long-distance airliner, balancing range with payload and passenger comfort

domestic wages. The Russians had also complained to the Germans about some of Junkers' methods and, in a severe ensuing move, all existing credit arrangements with the firm were stopped by the German government and the company was asked for repayment. For a while Junkers soldiered on, burdened by the repayments, but finally, on 3 October 1925, Junkers Flugzeugwerke AG ran out of money. The government offered a final subsidy, but in return for 66 per cent of Junkers Flugzeugwerke's shares and 80 per cent of the stock in the Junkers-Luftverkehrs airline. The following year, Junkers-Luftverkehrs merged with Deutscher Aero Lloyd and the Deutsch-Russische Luftverkehrsgesellschaft to form a new national airline, Deutsche Lufthansa (DLH).

For his part, throughout 1926, Hugo Junkers, now 67 years of age, felt himself to be a victim of intimidation and he became increasingly embittered and hostile towards those in authority who he thought had conspired against him. He struggled to retain control of what remained of his interests, but in December he reached an arrangement with the government in which he reacquired the shareholding in Junkers Flugzeugwerke and Jumo Motorenwerke he had lost the previous year. In return, he agreed to sell the remaining 20 per cent shareholding in the Junkers airline to the government and to repay 1 million Reichsmarks. He was also committed to supplying aircraft worth 2.7 million Reichsmarks.

From all this upheaval, Junkers had managed to regain control of his aircraft design and manufacturing business, at a time when the F 13 was the bestselling aircraft in Germany. In 1928, Junkers rolled out its 1000th aircraft, which happened to be a J 31 (G 31), a three-engined transport that was effectively an enlarged version of the G 24 and which was designed to operate as a freighter, a night-flying airliner with beds, toilet and even air conditioning, or as an air ambulance, but with all such internal equipment removable if required. With a wider, higher fuselage than the G 24, passengers could be served in-flight meals, hence the aircraft's moniker of 'the 'Flying Dining Car'.

Much of the impetus for Hugo Junkers' decision to develop a new, state-of-the-art transport aircraft and airliner had come from the opinions and experiences of senior executives employed by Junkers-Luftverkehr. Hans-Martin Bongers, a finance man who had once worked for the airline before joining Luft Hansa in 1929, told Junkers that he believed there would be significant growth in the number of airlines and the international routes on which they operated. Dipl.-Ing Kurt Weil, one-time Technical Director of the Junkers airline, had conducted detailed analysis of the business and, following his direct experience of operations in the Middle East, stressed to Professor Junkers the need for future airliners to be able to work from primitive conditions as routes expanded to take in poorer nations with less infrastructure.

Also growing was the air freight sector, and the managing director of Junkers-Luftverkehr, former 31-victory naval fighter ace and *Pour le Mérite*-holder Gotthard Sachsenberg, expressed his belief to Junkers that more freight companies should be established, but free of government control through the removal of subsidies. Sachsenberg also believed that the ideal transport aircraft should be a singled-engined machine, rather than three-engined, in order to save cost and to ease maintenance.

Indeed, Hugo Junkers had targeted the need to supply the growing market for transport aircraft as being the way ahead for his business, possibly even for its survival, and in 1928 he had approached Ernst Zindel to come up with a design for a new, larger transport that would improve on the G 24 and the G 31, but that would be inexpensive to build, be able to carry a payload of 2000 kg, be easy to maintain and be able to operate from grass airfields. To achieve this, Zindel believed that the optimum design should be for a single-engined aircraft, thus going against the existing trend for three-engined machines, such as the G 24. Junkers had already enjoyed success with single-engined, all-metal types, the firm's W 33 having set a world long-distance flying record and made the first non-stop flight from Europe to North America, while the W 34 would go on to claim a high-altitude record in 1929.

Under the project designation 'EF 30', Zindel thus pressed ahead with a single-engined design, the justification lying primarily in cost saving through the use of only one engine, which would, in turn, inherently reduce maintenance levels. He drew heavily from the G 24 and the G 31, but in essence the new design would emerge as an enlarged W 33/34.

It was planned to provide power from the new 750 hp Junkers L 88 engine, but this unit was still under development by the time Zindel got to work, and so he relied instead on the BMW VIIaU 680 hp water-cooled engine that could achieve a cruising speed of 160 km/h and a maximum speed of 190 km/h.

The 'EF 30' evolved as a low-wing cantilever monoplane with the tubular centre section being integrated with the fuselage. The box-like fuselage was formed of Duralumin longerons and transverse frames offering a main freight hold of 6.4 m in length, 1.61 m wide and 1.91 m maximum height, with large-area sidewalls, providing capacity of 16.7 m³. Zindel recalled of his design;

'The single-engined special cargo variant was characterised, notably, by a large 1.6 m wide and 1.5 m high hatch towards the rear end of the fuselage side, with a loading ramp incorporated, accessible behind the wing trailing edge and flaps. In the fuselage roof there was a large, 1.5 m x 1.2 m hatch for loading heavy, bulky loads from above by means of a crane. Entry for the crew was via a door behind the cockpit.'

The fuselage side hatch described by Zindel was double-doored and when opened, the lower door was designed to be low enough to allow loading to and from lorries. Another four, smaller, cargo compartments were built in below the floor, aft of the fuselage hatch. Zindel further recorded;

'The wings, as with earlier types, were fitted with twin flaps and ailerons in order to increase the maximum lift during takeoff and landing. With a payload of 2000 kg and range of about 1200 km, the takeoff weight of the single-engined aircraft was 7000 kg. With a wingspan of 29.5 m and

The prototype Ju 52/1mbe Wk-Nr 4001 D-1974 photographed at Berlin-Tempelhof in February 1931. The aircraft is fitted with a single BMW VIIaU 680 hp water-cooled engine, to which was mounted a four-bladed propeller as seen here. The aircraft's right-side fuselage door is open, as is the large roof hatch, which, together with window hatches and wide loading bay on the left side of the fuselage, demonstrate the flexibility and multi-access benefit of Zindel's design

a wing area of 100 m², the takeoff wing-loading was about 64 kg/m² and the landing speed 82 km/h. Since this machine also had quite slow landing characteristics and a sturdy undercarriage, it was easy to take off and land on the average kind of grass surfaces, which, for a freight aircraft, was of considerable importance.'

Indeed, when the flaps were lowered, the ailerons automatically dropped, which assisted with low takeoff and landing speeds. The tailplane was braced and the undercarriage was installed with oil-filled shock absorbers in each wheel strut, with struts from each wheel being braced to the fuselage underside. The undercarriage was designed to be changed for floats or skis. Similarly, a swivelling tailwheel was fitted, also with a shock absorber.

Construction based on Zindel's design commenced in 1929 under the type designation 'Ju 52' and, despite going against the suggestions and recommendations of senior air transport figures for passenger accommodation, it was to be, exclusively, a freight aircraft. Zindel was satisfied and unapologetic;

'We succeeded in designing a satisfactory and uniform basic design for fuselage, wings and tailplanes for both purposes, even though the design for a passenger aeroplane would have resulted in a slightly more favourable solution [number of passengers, cabin size].'

Junkers advertised its new machine as 'a single-engined freight aeroplane Junkers Ju 52 with large lateral hinged door and upper loading hatch'.

On 11 September 1930, the prototype 'Ju 52/1m' ('1m' standing for '1 motor') Wk-Nr 4001 took off from Dessau flown by company test pilot Flugkapitän Wilhelm Zimmermann. The flight went well and resulted in some minor improvements to the aircraft, with the rudder area being increased and adjustments made to the mass balancing of the elevators. The aircraft was then moved to the Deutsche Versuchsanstalt für Luftfahrt (DVL – German Experimental Institute for Aviation) at Berlin-Adlershof for more tests. It remained there until 10 February 1931, when test-flying was finally resumed, by which stage it had been assigned the code D-1974. The Ju 52/1m was unveiled to the public at Berlin-Tempelhof airfield a week later, and the following summer it made a 6000-km promotional flight from Budapest to Prague, stopping at Bucharest, Sofia, Belgrade, Athens and Vienna en route.

A second Ju 52/1m, Wk-Nr 4002 D-2133, was completed in January 1931. For this aircraft Junkers resorted to using the 800 hp, 14-cylinder, twin-row, air-cooled, Leopard radial engine made by the British firm of Armstrong Siddeley. Zindel recorded how, 'The second available engine of equivalent power [to the L 88] was the Leopard, which was equipped with a reduction gear for the propeller shaft. When selling the aircraft to foreign customers it was fortunate that in addition to the German water-cooled engine, there was an English air-cooled engine from the prestigious firm of Amstrong-Siddeley'.

However, the 'fortunate' availability of the Leopard may have been one thing, but in reality, its performance on the Ju 52/1m was another. The Leopard-fitted aircraft failed to start on its planned maiden flight, and it was not until a specialist from Armstrong Siddeley arrived to fix the problem that it eventually took to the air in mid-April, when it flew as a Ju 52/1mbi with the Leopard uncowled. The aircraft was re-designated as the Ju 52/1mci when it was fitted with a pair of 11.5 m-long floats at Rosslau, north of Dessau, to assess its potential as a maritime machine. Wilhelm Zimmermann flew the Junkers on its trial seaplane flight over the river Elbe, and a few weeks later it was moved to the maritime aircraft test centre at Travemünde, where it gave a mediocre performance. Subsequently, its floats were removed, having been found to be too curved, and D-2133 reverted to a landplane configuration to be known as the Ju 52/1mdi.

Intriguingly, during the 1930s, one German aviation journalist described the Ju 52/1m as being a 'single-engined large freight aircraft with base and side loading ports', with 'seating room for 17 passengers and two-three seats for pilot and navigator'.

Ultimately, only one Ju 52/1m was sold to a foreign customer. Wk-Nr 4006 was disassembled in Germany and shipped to Canada, where it was utilised by Canadian Airways. The aircraft was reassembled by the Fairchild Aviation Company in Montreal and fitted at first with an Armstrong Siddeley Leopard. It then made flights over eastern Canada and the northeastern US states. The Leopard had to be removed when it suffered from the harsh climate of far North America, its replacement being a BMW VIIa, but that engine fared little better and required regular maintenance. The Junkers is believed to have undertaken supply flights to remote trapper stations along the Hudson Bay, and it carried cargoes of dynamite, ore buckets and lumber for mining companies and dam builders. It also flew in furs and fish for collection at rail junctions.

Known as the 'White Elephant' and the 'Flying Boxcar', it was the largest aircraft in Canada at the time. It later flew with Canadian Pacific (which purchased Canadian Airways in 1941), who operated it with wheels, floats and skis with few difficulties. It was eventually fitted with an 825 hp 12-cylinder, liquid-cooled, Rolls-Royce Buzzard inline engine, Junkers classifying the machine as the Ju 52/1mcao. However, by the time the Buzzard was reaching the end of its serviceable life, the ship carrying five replacement engines from England was sunk by a U-boat and Canadian Pacific removed the aircraft from service in 1943. It ended its days in Winnipeg, Manitoba, where it was eventually scrapped in 1947.

Ground personnel close the left-side window and roof hatches on Ju 52/1m Wk-Nr 4001 D-1974. This image shows to good effect the considerable stowage space offered by the aircraft, as well as the bulk and weight of single items that it could accommodate, as evidenced by the large, wooden crate just inside the main loading hatch. The hatch was designed so that large items could be easily transferred to and from vehicles

In the meantime, the Junkers team had become frustrated by the lack of favourable response to, or orders generated from, the publicity trip made by D-1974. Zindel wrote, 'the single-engined freight version of the Ju 52 did not sell as well as anticipated, especially as the grand airfreight plans of the former Junkers air transport experts never materialised, essentially because time and conditions were not ready for their philosophies'.

But at least the firm was able to replace the BMW VIIaU on D-1974 with the intended Junkers L88 engine which had finally become available. A four-bladed wooden propeller was fitted and a large radiator was installed to the underside of the nose. Additionally, new, stronger wings were installed which were more swept back, these being matched by a fortified undercarriage. So improved, the 'Ju 52/1mbe' took to the skies on 6 September 1931. In January 1932, however, the BMW engine was refitted and drag flaps added as the Ju 52/1mca. Later the aircraft was fitted with the Junkers 750 hp Jumo 4 Diesel engine (re-designated as the Jumo 204 later in the year) for testing.

Yet even as albeit limited production of the Ju 52/1m was under way, Professor Junkers and Ernst Zindel knew that they would have to adapt their design. Shortly before embarking on the 'EF 30' project, Junkers had carried out a survey of senior figures within the airline industry, such as the ambitious Operations Director of Luft Hansa, Erhard Milch, whose opinions were becoming increasingly influential, and from it they concluded that the broad consensus of opinion was that a multi-engine machine was what was needed. Milch and his fellow executives were looking for a design that bettered considerably the G 24. They were looking for a '*Schnellverkehrs-Großflugzeug*' (high-speed large transport aircraft). Furthermore, Dr. Erich Schatzki, head of Luft Hansa's *Technische Entwicklungsabteilung* (Technical Development Department) and a former test pilot for the airline, suggested that the Ju 52 could be adapted to take three engines. Hugo Junkers took exception to this, declaring, 'We don't have to toe Luft Hansa's line!'

But, in fact, Zindel had already started paving the way. In April 1931 he had overseen the installation of dummy, engineless nacelles with twin-bladed propellers fitted to each wing of a Ju 52/1m in order to assess

Ju 52/1m Wk-Nr 4006 CF-ARM was fitted with skis and operated by Canadian Pacific Airways from 1936 amidst the freezing conditions of eastern Canada. The aircraft was used to carry supplies for mining and lumber firms and continued to fly in North America until 1943

drag – something that had already been attempted on an F 13. Yet the Ju 52 presented no real problems when it came to adding new engines and, aside from minor strengthening of the wings and undercarriage in order to take the increase in weight and speed, it proved relatively straightforward to create a three-engined aircraft using the basic airframe of the 1m. Additionally, the upgrade in design necessitated an expansion to the tail fin, as well as inclusion of an adjustable vertical rudder relief in case of asymmetrical twin-engined flight, and rubber cables to operate the cockpit foot pedals.

Based on the Pratt & Whitney nine-cylinder Hornet radial engine, the planned air-cooled BMW 132 wing engines were to be canted outwards slightly so that directional stability could be maintained if one engine suffered failure. Mounted on removable Duralumin tube bearers, they were secured by safety cables fastened loosely around the cylinders and tied behind the firewall that would prevent them from becoming detached if and when subjected to propeller damage or collision. Fuel was held in five light metal wing tanks, with each wing holding 2000 litres that was pumped by Junkers-manufactured pumps. There was an emergency gravity tank and a cockpit hand pump, as well as jettisoning valves in the wings. Each engine could be regulated for standard and high-altitude performance, with cowling adjustment, oil-cooler control and an oil shut-off valve.

Meanwhile, although it seemed little appeal remained for the Ju 52/1m, in 1932 Bolivian airline Lloyd Aero Boliviano (LAB) expressed an interest in the proposed 3m, and, grasping at this, Junkers quickly set about converting Wk-Nrs 4008 and 4009 to a tri-motor configuration in the hope of gaining a customer.

In early air tests, however, problems with drag did occur as a result of three engines, along with high air resistance. Zindel and the technicians from BMW went back to the drawing board and re-engineered the design to incorporate a cowling ring, influenced by the British Townend ring, which was fitted around the air-cooled cylinders of the centre engine to reduce drag but maintain cooling. Additionally, following tests in the Junkers wind tunnel, cladding over the undercarriage struts was streamlined, and these measures resulted in a reduction of drag area.

The problems were solved and in early 1932 LAB placed a firm order for the aircraft. Accordingly, further flight-testing was carried out in March with Wk-Nr 4008 fitted with three 550 hp Hornet engines licence-built by BMW. On the 7th, the Ju 52/3m took to the air for the first time, attaining speeds of around 230 km/h. With a somewhat rushed process of testing completed, Wk-Nr 4008 was disassembled and crated for shipment to Bolivia. When it arrived there it was registered as CB-17 and named *JUAN DE VALLE*. The aeroplane was followed by Wk-Nr 4009, which was coded CB-18 and named *HUANUNI*. These two aircraft were destined for much more demanding work than anticipated.

From December 1928, Bolivia and Paraguay had been in dispute over possession of the Gran Chaco, a vast, hostile and sparsely-populated desert region spanning the border areas of the two countries. Though neither country had settled more than the territory immediately adjoining their own frontiers, both laid claim to the whole region. Oil was a main ingredient

The Ju 52/3m was pressed into service as a military aircraft for the first time in the early 1930s during the Chaco War between Bolivia and Paraguay. The *Fuerza Aérea Boliviana* used its three Ju 52/3ms to transport and airdrop weapons and supplies to troops fighting in remote jungle areas, as well as on crudely conducted bombing operations. After the conflict, the Junkers returned to the role of airliner with Lloyd Aero Boliviano. Here, wounded men are being airlifted using Ju 52/3m Wk-Nr 4018 *CHOROLQUE*

in the escalation of a stand-off to full-scale war – oilfields had been discovered in Bolivian territory, close to the western extremity of the Chaco where the US Standard Oil Company had been extracting small quantities of oil near Villa Montes since the 1920s. But this, if anything, was merely one spark that ignited the flame. For its part, Paraguay viewed Bolivian advances towards its border as a threat to its national existence.

Clashes at border posts became a regular occurrence and both Bolivia and Paraguay constructed lines of fortifications across the Chaco. In June 1932, a Bolivian patrol captured a Paraguayan fort. This triggered an escalation in the conflict and the belligerents eventually became bogged down in what would become the 'Chaco War', Latin America's bloodiest 20th-century conflict.

Throughout the war, although aircraft generally played a minor role, both nations attempted to expand their respective air forces. However, this was set against a background of embargoes initiated by the League of Nations, difficulties associated with shipping and transport, the land-locked locations of the countries, and the challenges of training and maintenance. Bolivia placed most emphasis on air operations and attempted to equip its air arm, the *Fuerza Aérea Boliviana* (FAB), with the best aircraft it could afford and obtain, including British, French and American machines. But, whilst Bolivia may have been the stronger power, its forces were frequently outmanoeuvred and outfought by the Paraguayans.

When the Ju 52/3ms destined for LAB arrived in Bolivia, they were quickly taken over by the military, had camouflage schemes and FAB markings applied, and were pressed into service for military operations, mainly to fly twice-daily air supply drops to trapped Bolivian troops in the Chaco region. Such flights were extremely hazardous, conducted at low level under baking hot skies or in bad weather, and often in the face of enemy ground fire. In hours of darkness the temperature would fall by 40 degrees, compelling crews to drain oil from the engines at night to prevent it from freezing and causing damage. Yet, the sight of a Ju 52/3m arriving at a remote airstrip from the rear, laden with supplies, signalled to beleaguered troops hope and relief, and, for the wounded, escape via airlift.

The aircraft's sturdy metal construction was well suited to the primitive, mountainous airstrips, where fuel would usually have to be hand-pumped into the wing tanks, a procedure that took hours. But it was an impossible task for two Junkers to drop the amount of supplies needed to keep thousands of cut-off men provided with food, water, ammunition and general equipment. Eventually, in September 1932, a third Ju 52/3m, Wk-Nr 4018, named *CHOROLQUE*, arrived, which offered a marginal increase in capacity and the rate of supply flights and drops. With local lessons learned, this aircraft came fitted with more fuselage windows and ventilation inlets.

A US military observer on the Bolivian side noted how 'aviation played a very insignificant part in the war. Observation was difficult, due to the thickly wooded areas. Attempts were made at attack and bombardment, but results were unsatisfactory. The greatest number of casualties in the air forces occurred from accidents, however. The pilots as a whole were not well trained and demonstrated little initiative and courage. The most effective results were obtained by the air force in observation and transport. The Bolivians used a Junkers Ju 52/3m on one occasion to transport two complete batteries of artillery – one of 75 mm and one of 105 mm – one gun being carried at a time, and with each 75 mm piece, the gun crew and considerable ammunition. The tri-motor Ju 52s were used to a considerable extent in evacuating the sick and wounded'.

In September 1932, Ju 52/3m Wk-Nr 4018 *CHOROLQUE* became the third Junkers to be acquired by the Bolivians. After service in the Chaco War, it was redeployed as an airliner with Lloyd Aero Boliviano, and it is seen here in its peacetime role

The Junkers were also pressed into service as 'bombers', and during such missions the crew simply threw bombs out of the fuselage side windows down onto Paraguayan positions.

Finally, following the loss of 100,000 men in a war that had almost destroyed both nations, in June 1935 a ceasefire was declared. Over a period of three years, the three Ju 52/3ms had ferried some 40,000 Bolivian troops and 4850 tons of supplies and, contrary to the American attaché's report, at least as far as the Ju 52/3ms were concerned, without an accident. Dan Hagedorn, a historian specialising in Latin American aviation, has noted that the Ju 52/3m's 'value to the Bolivian cause cannot be overstated'.

With the end of the Chaco War, the Ju 52/3ms were quickly returned to LAB, which deployed them on its commercial routes over vast forests and jungles, often operating from aerodromes some 4000 m above sea level. Flights frequently crossed the northern Andes at 7300 m, and at such altitude the Ju 52/3m's double-wing ailerons, flaps and elevators were highly valued. Indeed, such was the airline's opinion of the Junkers that it made an order for a fourth machine. Wk-Nr 4061 was subsequently shipped to Bolivia and saw service with LAB as CB-21 *BOLIVAR*.

The performance of the Ju 52/3m in Bolivia prompted further interest from South America, and an order was placed by the Colombian *Aviación Militar*. It used three upgraded Ju 52/1ms to ferry troops and supplies to a remote Amazonian region known as the Leticia quadrilateral or trapezium following a border clash with neighbouring Peru in 1932-33. Peruvian forces had occupied the key Colombian port of Leticia in what became known as the 'Leticia Incident' and the region stood on the brink of major conflict. Both the Colombians and the Peruvians needed reliable aircraft, ideally able to operate on water. The three converted 1ms were fitted with floats and flew equipment and supplies from Barranquilla. This time, however, in July 1933, the League of Nations managed to negotiate the return of Leticia and the surrounding area to Colombian control, thus averting a further escalation of the conflict.

An excellent view of the distinctively finished Ju 52/3mge, Wk-Nr 5020 D-AZIS *HORST WESSEL*, which was operated by the *Regierungsstaffel*, or 'government squadron'. Named after a young Berlin *Sturmabteilung* (SA) leader who died in February 1930 after having been attacked by Communists, D-AZIS was the aircraft of the SA Chief of Staff, Obergruppenführer Viktor Lutze, during the late 1930s. The colour of the aircraft was probably intended to be representative of the 'brownshirts', and the emblem on the wings was that of the SA

Ju 52/3m D-ANYK *WILHELM SCHMID* forms one of a group of Lufthansa machines outside the hangars at Berlin-Tempelhof. This aircraft has its engines tarpaulined, suggesting that it has not been used for some time. D-ANYK would eventually operate over China with the Eurasia Aircraft Corporation, where it was re-coded EU-XV. The aeroplane was subsequently destroyed in a Japanese bombing raid

In Germany, Junkers was buoyed by more orders for the Ju 52/3m from Finland, which would eventually take three aircraft for use by its national airline, Aero O/Y, and neighbouring Sweden, which took a sole float-fitted example. But these early, encouraging, signs would be dwarfed by the ambition and scale of Luft Hansa's development and expansion under the Nazi government in the 1930s. During the second half of that decade, Nazi Germany fostered a sense of 'air-mindedness', creating and developing an ever-expanding infrastructure of state sponsored flying schools and aero-clubs, as well as encouraging aircraft and aircraft engine manufacturers and aero-industry companies to increase production on an unprecedented scale. The Nazis also attached considerable importance to the development of commercial aviation.

Deutsche Luft Hansa Aktiengesellschaft (DLH) was formed in Berlin in January 1926 from the merger of Junkers-Luftverkehr and Deutscher Aero Lloyd which operated airline services across Europe. The merger had not been a particularly happy affair, with Professor Junkers accepting it reluctantly and only under bully-boy pressure and tactics used by Ernst Brandenburg at the Ministry of Transport, who wanted to emulate the British example of a single, leading, domestic and international 'flag carrier'.

At the helm of DLH, Erhard Milch, in accordance with Brandenburg's policy, rationalised the airline's fleet and introduced efficient working procedures aimed at optimising efficiency and profit. His view was that aircraft made money when they were flying, not on the ground, irrespective of light or darkness, or of good or bad weather. As such, he was attracted to multi-engined aircraft which offered greater range, and he began to invest in a network of radio navigational beacons, as well as instrument training for pilots. Under Milch's leadership, DLH grew to become the most important airline in Europe, its aircraft flying farther and carrying more passengers than its British, French and Italian competitors. He and Brandenburg also worked closely with the Defence Ministry, which covertly placed men with the airline for training for future military deployment.

Milch also understood that the customer was the prime consideration – as such the company had already placed the emphasis on comfort. In 1928 stewards had been introduced to serve drinks and snacks on some G 31 flights, and reclining seats were added to the twin-engined Albatros L 73 biplane. Strangely, however, as the airline achieved greater efficiency, the superior levels of passenger comfort it provided sometimes worked against it, and there were complaints from customers if their aircraft arrived early at their destination!

On 15 June 1932, Luft Hansa test pilot Willy Polte flew the Ju 52/3m to evaluate it, and his subsequent report was so positive that Milch ordered more aircraft. The first two machines to be delivered to the airline were the 440 hp BMW Hornet radial-powered Ju 52/3mce Wk-Nr 4013 D-2201, named *BOELCKE*, and Ju 52/3mce Wk-Nr 4015 D-2202, named *RICHTHOFEN*. When tested, these aircraft also proved very satisfactory. Even the *Führer*'s personal pilot, Hans Baur, flew one of the early machines and found the Ju 52/3m to offer a major improvement over other transport aircraft of the time.

Also in 1932, DLH commenced using the Ju 52/3m on its Berlin–London, Berlin–Rome and Munich–Vienna routes, as well as on its night service from Berlin to Königsberg. By the end of the year, DLH operated more than 1930 km of scheduled night routes, and in the following year a further 961 km would be added. Some aircraft were deployed on the overnight Berlin–Königsberg freight flights by the *Deutsche Reichsbahn* and by DLH on 'railway connection' flights. There is some belief that this scheme was also intended as a cover to train up future bomber crews. As a final endorsement, from June 1933 Adolf Hitler took on Ju 52/3mfe Wk-Nr 4021 D-2600 *IMMELMANN* as his personal aircraft until 1937.

DLH was now lodged firmly in day-to-day German life, its aircraft having become ubiquitous, and yet air travel was seen as glamorous. The route network was expanding and timetables became more regular. The airline featured in newspapers, magazines and at the cinema. DLH's four leading test pilots had flown one million transport flight-kilometres and the press dubbed them the 'Flying millionaires of the air'.

Prior to 1933, however, the reality was that Junkers was able to produce just 18 Ju 52/3ms per

Ten of Lufthansa's Ju 52/3ms parked on the apron at Berlin-Tempelhof. After the Nazi Party came to power in 1933, the trend was to name such aircraft after prominent figures associated with the Party or in honour of accomplished wartime pilots, such as Kleine, Boelke, Büchner, Dostler and Göring as seen here. The farthest machine in the centre row, Wk-Nr 5180 D-ALYL *HANS LOEB*, carries markings to commemorate the 1936 Berlin Olympic Games

Lufthansa mechanics service the right-hand BMW 132 radial engine of Ju 52/3m Wk-Nr 4029 D-2650 *FRITZ RUMEY*, which was later transferred to the Luftwaffe. The double 'gull wing' panels allowed good, clear access for maintenance

Ju 52/3m Wk-Nr 5610 OY-DAL *SELANDIA* was operated by the Danish airline Det Danske Luftfartselskab A/S on its routes between Copenhagen and Stockholm, Malmö, Hamburg, Berlin, Amsterdam, Rotterdam, Brussels, Antwerp, Paris and London

year as long as production ceased on all other types. On 22 August of that year Milch informed Hugo Junkers' son, Klaus, the managing director of Junkers Flugzeugwerke AG, that Dessau would be given a contract for 1000 Ju 52/3ms, with the first 178 of them to be delivered in 1934. The Ju 52/3m duly entered series manufacture, and, by the summer of 1935, the aircraft accounted for approximately 85 per cent of the DLH fleet. Indeed, one member of the Lufthansa board (the company had become known by the one-word 'Lufthansa' in the summer of 1933) commented, 'One of the most noticeable milestones of the year 1935 will be the use of Ju 52 aircraft, which will form the mainstay of four-fifths of German air traffic flown over Lufthansa-covered routes. The older aircraft types will disappear almost completely, so that Deutsche Lufthansa's comprehensive procurement programme is now concluded'.

From Berlin, where the vast Tempelhof airport with its extended runways and ultra-modern architecture, known as the '*Luftkreuz Europas*' (Europe's air crossroads), represented the state of the art in air travel, DLH's Junkers flew progressively over an expanding domestic route network. Ju 52/3ms of many other nations – Austria, Belgium, Denmark, Hungary, Poland, Sweden and Switzerland – also gave Tempelhof a distinctly international atmosphere. Air mail increased dramatically from 748 tons in 1934 to 1408 tons in 1935. As one example of the increase in passenger traffic, in 1936 Rhein-Main airport handled 58,010 passengers and 796 tons of mail, along with 801 tons of freight on 5270 flights, while the following year, these volumes increased to 70,910 passengers and 7090 flights, respectively, along with 1452 tons of mail and 966 tons of freight.

By 10 January 1936, 787 Ju 52/3ms had been built, and, by 31 March, this figure had climbed to 839, with another 153 arriving between then and 31 March 1938. The aircraft were becoming increasingly sophisticated too. The Ju 52/3mnai supplied to Sweden's AB Aerotransport for service on the Stockholm–Malmö and Stockholm–Amsterdam/Copenhagen/London/Paris routes, was installed with three Pratt & Whitney Wasp nine-cylinder, air-cooled radial engines with NACA cowlings which, although having about the same power as the BMWs, offered better takeoff, climbing and cruising performance and a greatly improved range, increasing from 920 km to 1160 km. Engine vibration was reduced by the fitting of better mountings, and the cowlings were fitted with snap-fasteners to allow quick inspection. Fuel tankage also increased to 2470 litres, which resulted in a stronger undercarriage being installed.

Internally, the cockpit saw improvement with new radio equipment, a redesigned instrument panel, more warning lights, a gyro horizon and a precision altimeter. Both the cockpit and the passenger cabin benefited from an improved heating system, and passengers also enjoyed Kapok

Ju 52/3mge Wk-Nr 4074 D-ASIS *WILHELM CUNO* of Lufthansa on the concrete at Croydon Airport, in England, during the mid-1930s. The airline's flag flies from the cockpit

soundproofing, leather upholstered seats, better carpeting, grain panelling, polished fittings, diffused overhead lighting, greater baggage capacity and a water-drained WC.

Export orders came from all over the world, including Argentina, Australia, Austria, Belgium, Brazil, China, Denmark, Ecuador, Great Britain, Greece, Hungary, Italy, Lebanon, Mexico, Mozambique, Norway, Peru, Poland, Portugal, South Africa and Spain. But, in contrast, the year 1937 saw production activity plateau. Only a few Ju 52/3ms were sold abroad, and of all the main aircraft types being operated in Germany, both civil and military, the Ju 52/3m proved the most costly. At the end of 1937, the Air Ministry's Production Plan Nr 7 called for the output of just 100 Ju 52/3ms in 1938 – a figure reflecting the growing importance of the Ju 88 bomber programme. Paradoxically, however, by 1938 it was largely the Ju 52/3m, and Milch's direction, which had pushed DLH into becoming one of the world's premier airlines. In the year ending 31 March 1938, it had carried 177,000 passengers and in 1939 its European routes stretched from London to Istanbul and from Lisbon to Helsinki.

Yet in the late 1930s, as the airline networks expanded and became ever more sophisticated, so political events in parts of Europe were becoming ever more precarious. One such place of unrest was Spain, and it would be there that the Ju 52/3m would be called upon to undertake new and more warlike tasks.

Ju 52/3mge Wk-Nr 4057 ZS-AFB *Lord Charles Somerset* of South West African Airways flies past the dramatic scenery of Lion's Head mountain in Cape Town in December 1934. The aircraft was one of eight Ju 52/3ms operated by South African airlines

Ju 52/3m 22•90 of 2.K/88 jacked up during maintenance at a forward airfield. The dorsal turret has been covered by a tarpaulin and the right side engine appears to have been removed, leaving just the cowling in place. The small emblem on the cowling may connect the aircraft to 7./KG 153, which operated Ju 52/3ms up to the spring of 1937. The nose engine also lacks a propeller

CHAPTER TWO

SPANISH SKIES

Hugo Junkers never saw his Ju 52/3m go to war. Shortly after the Nazi Party took power in Germany, there were those amongst its hierarchy who had become easily convinced that Junkers had supposedly mixed with left-wing, Jewish and liberal groups – a situation that was unacceptable to the Aviation Minister Hermann Göring. This state of affairs gave Milch the justification to set about a deliberate campaign of pressure against Junkers, following the ageing industrialist's resistance to Milch's demanding production programmes.

In March 1933, Göring and Milch requested that Professor Junkers release his patents and place his factories at the disposal of the State in order to sustain its rearmament programme. Then they demanded that he withdraw his involvement with the company before any further contracts from the Ministry of Aviation (*Reichsluftfahrtministerium* – RLM) would be forthcoming. At this, Junkers left for his home in Bavaria and prepared to fight it out. At first, Milch agreed that Junkers could continue with his experimental work, but also insisted that the patents and the factories were needed by the Reich. He impressed upon Junkers that he should display some acknowledgement of the fact that without RLM subsidies his business would not have stood much chance of surviving anyway. Junkers remained defiant.

In October, the RLM presented Junkers with an ultimatum – the choice was to either sell his controlling stakes in his two companies or accept being banned from any further involvement with his factories. Furthermore, if Junkers did not accede, his dealings in the Soviet Union during the 1920s would be investigated under suspicion of financial misconduct. So it was that Milch ensured that every detail of the mismanagement that had taken place was made public. Junkers was taken from his home under police escort on charges of treason and moved to Dessau, where the Nazis carried out their investigation and also threatened him with legal action.

Junkers finally gave in and at the end of October, he sold the bulk of his interests in his businesses to the Reich, as well as resigning his directorships. This having been done, he was ordered back to Bavaria, where he was placed under house arrest. In February 1934 Junkers consented to sell the residual holdings in his companies and the arrest order was lifted. When Junkers eventually died at his home on 3 February 1935, Milch, hypocritically, sent a wreath. On 3 April that year the Junkers companies were nationalised and effectively placed under the control of the RLM under the direction of Heinrich Koppenberg, who had been appointed by Milch.

In January 1934, at the time Hugo Junkers was suffering from Göring's and Milch's persecution, DLH was instructed by Milch to make available some of its Ju 52/3m airliners to the Luftwaffe, along with a small, selected group of its ground personnel. Conveniently, the Luftwaffe's first bomber unit, *Bombengeschwader* (BG) 1, was based at DLH's Tempelhof hub. Indeed, this unit had been hidden from the eyes of the Versailles inspectors within the innocently titled 'DLH Transport Inspectorate'. Under conditions of the greatest secrecy, the aircraft were prepared so that they could be rapidly modified as basic bombers using *Schnellrüstsätzen* (quick conversion kits), with most conversion work being undertaken by Weser-Flugzeugbau. Military pilots flew in the transport role with the DLH Training School to gain experience on multi-engined types, while radio equipment was purchased and stored quietly at a number of locations around the Reich. By March 1934, however, when the cloak of secrecy over German aeronautical activity had been lifted, the Inspectorate had received 24 Ju 52/3ms and three Dornier Do 11s.

This development caused some surprise at Dessau. Ernst Zindel recalled the situation affecting both bomber aircraft development shortly after the Nazi Party came to power and the Junkers Flugzeugwerke's position;

'Although other companies had made various bomber prototypes, it was realised that no suitable aircraft existed which could be developed into series production. A few years previously, a commission from the *Heereswaffenamt* (Army Ordnance Office) made a fact-finding visit to Junkers at Dessau and made a damning indictment of the Ju 52, noting, disapprovingly, that as a bomber it would be completely unsuitable. But since that time, Erhard Milch, on a whim and now employed in the newly formed RLM, decided to turn the Ju 52, which had proved itself so well as a peace time aircraft, into a "*Behelfsbomber*" (Auxiliary Bomber)! Nobody at Junkers had contemplated such a development, and all considerations had been directed towards the deployment of both the single-engined transport aircraft and the three-engined passenger aircraft exclusively for use in times of peace.

'In reality, the usual means of accommodation, or even the horizontal suspension of small 50 kg bombs in the Ju 52's large fuselage, was really

Professor Hugo Junkers and his wife, Therese, enjoy a stroll in the sun at Baden-Baden in 1934. Towards the end of his life, Junkers became the victim of machinations by the Secretary of State for Aviation, Erhard Milch, and others, who wanted to assume nationalised control of the Junkers companies. These actions had their effect on Junkers and he died at home in Bavaria on 3 February 1935

Freshly manufactured ESAC 25/IX vertical bomb stowage cells. These electrically-operated cells were fitted into the Ju 52/3m to convert the airliner-cum-transport into a *Behelfsbomber*

The ventral 'dustbin' turret, as fitted to the Ju 52/3m. It is seen here extended beneath the corrugated metal fuselage and fitted in standard configuration with a 7.92 mm MG 15 machine gun. The turret proved questionable, both in terms of operation and the level of defence it provided. It was exposed and dangerous for the gunner and induced drag. The turret was withdrawn from later Ju 52/3ms

not at all suitable and the bombs would be restricted by the limited space between the four main, low-wing, cross-spars of the Ju 52/3m's wing centre section, which traversed the fuselage at gaps of just 800 mm. Never for a moment did we intend for the Ju 52 to be used for military purposes.'

The pressing of the Ju 52/3m into service as a *Behelfsbomber* came about essentially because at the time the RLM had little choice. The only dedicated bomber in service in 1934 was the Do 11, an outdated angular, shoulder-wing monoplane available in small numbers and powered by two 650 hp Siemens radial engines. It featured the first retractable undercarriage to be fitted into such an aircraft, but it came with problems, ranging from mechanical unreliability to excessive vibration that brought on structural issues. Not for nothing did its crews refer to the Do 11 as the 'Flying Coffin'. Its replacement, the big, box-like Do 23 with its heavy, fixed, spatted undercarriage and open cockpits and gunners' positions, was almost a retrograde step, while the Do 19 was two years away from flying.

The Luftwaffe needed a reliable bomber available in numbers. As such, an expedient solution to the Ju 52/3m's inability to offer horizontal bomb stowage was found in the ESAC (*Elektrische Senkrechtaufhängung für Cylindrischebomben*) electrically-operated 250/IX suspension cell – a vertical bomb rack developed in the 1920s, six of which could be installed quite easily in three bomb-bays between the spaces in the Ju 52/3m's cross-members. They were able to hold a total of either six 250 kg SC 250 or 24 50 kg SC 50 *Minenbomben* (aerial mines) or 90 SC 10 *Splitterbomben* (fragmentation bombs). Provision was also possible for the carriage of 864 B 1E Electron incendiary bombs in a BSK 36 cluster canister.

To release the ordnance, the observer/ventral gunner would pull back a hatch in the floor. As Zindel recalled;

'Because the Luftwaffe wanted to commence series production quickly, but they had no suitable aircraft, the so-called "vertical suspension" method of carrying bombs, and the vertical dropping of bombs, was chosen as a quick-fix solution, but it was a solution that brought with it a certain deterioration in [bombing] accuracy.'

Six months after the formation of BG 1, the unit was divided into two *Behelfskampfgeschwader* (Auxiliary Bomber Wings), with BKG 172 at Tutow (which continued to be known by its DLH cover name) and BKG 274 in Berlin and at Fassberg, both units using the Ju 52/3m. In August 1934, a specialist 'radio direction research squadron' for the 'electronics industry' based at Tutow also took on Ju 52/3m *Behelfsbombers*.

This sudden appetite for converted Ju 52/3ms began to place some strain on the infrastructure at Dessau. The RLM's 1934 '*Rheinland*' production programme listed a requirement of no fewer than 450 Ju 52/3m 'bombers' between January 1934 and September 1935, a figure that exceeded those for the Do 11 (150) and the Do 13 (222). Zindel recorded;

'In 1934, in a very unusual move for the time, the Junkers aircraft works was contracted by the RLM for an accelerated production of a large series of such bombers – some 1200 machines, of which the number of machines produced monthly after start-up was to be in the order of 60.

'With this task set by the RLM, a completely new form of production technology and organisation was needed for the Junkers Flugzeugwerke. The plant management, under the leadership of Klaus Junkers, the second eldest son of Professor Junkers, together with the operations manager, Oberingenieur Thiedemann, and the works manager, Ing. Kuhnen, soon realised that only with completely new working methods and innovative streamlined production could the formidable production requirement be met and assured. We had to avoid becoming a "sweat shop" and so we introduced well-defined systems operating in carefully timed and scheduled cycles. In order not to place too many cycles on individual assembly lines and to avoid blockages and conflicts, production of the aircraft was broken down into separate modules. For example, the wings and fuselage would arrive pre-assembled as far as was possible, for final assembly only at the main joints.'

Despite Junkers' best efforts, however, Luftwaffe technicians still found fault with the Ju 52/3m's lack of speed, non-self-sealing fuel tanks, weak defensive armament and poor manoeuvrability, all of which combined to make it relatively easy prey to fighter attack.

In its *Behelfsbomber* configuration, the Ju 52/3m was fitted with a single Rheinmetall 7.9 mm MG 15 machine gun (with 1050 rounds) mounted in an open, dorsal-position just past the midway point heading aft along the top of the fuselage, while a similarly armed (750 rounds), semi-retractable, ventral, 'dustbin' turret was installed into the underside of the fuselage between the second and third bomb cells. The turret doubled up as an observation platform for the bombardier.

In June 1934 KG 154 'Boelcke' was established at Fassberg, its *Stabsstaffel* being drawn from elements of BKG 274. The *Stab* and II. *Gruppe* were mostly equipped with available Ju 52/3ms, while the first 193 Ju 52/3ms to be delivered from the '*Rheinland*' programme went to I./KG 154 and the new I./KG 252 (formed from elements of BKG 172), as well as to new bomber training schools at Lechfeld and Prenzlau. It was planned to produce 116 *Behelf* Ju 52/3ms between 1 October 1935 and 1 April 1936, allowing the formation of I. and II./KG 153 at Merseburg and Fürstenwalde. Although they had re-equipped with Dorniers by the end of 1935, the *Geschwaderstab* at Merseburg and a new III./KG 153 at Altenburg received Junkers tri-motors as well.

From April 1936 the Luftwaffe bomber force underwent a rapid expansion – III./KG 152 was formed at Greifswald with Ju 52/3ms, the *Gruppe* relocating to Barth in the summer, but recently formed I./KG 253 exchanged its Ju 52/3ms for Do 23s, while II. *Gruppe* continued to fly Junkers. II./KG 155 was established at Neukirchen, III./KG 155 at Schwäbisch Hall and I./KG 254 at

A formation of Luftwaffe Ju 52/3ms passes low overhead during the Nazi 'Party Day' at Nuremberg in September 1935 in a blatant display of freedom from the Treaty of Versailles. Examination of the photograph shows that these aircraft bear the code '42', meaning they are from KG 254, and that the ventral 'dustbin' turrets are lowered

Delmenhorst, all *Gruppen* equipped with the Ju 52/3m. IV./KG 153 also formed with Junkers at Liegnitz from March 1937. Thus, the solid, reliable, easy-to-fly aircraft would remain in production and continue to be used as a 'short-term' *Behelfsbomber* in order to plug gaps in the production programmes elsewhere. Yet the fact was that the Ju 52/3m, made of critically scarce Duralumin and powered by three engines, consumed more fuel than the twin-engined types.

SPANISH CIVIL WAR

On 17 July 1936 in Las Palmas, off the coast of the Spanish Sahara, Ju 52/3m Wk-Nr 5074 D-APOK *MAX VON MULZER*, flown by the record-breaking long-distance Lufthansa pilot, Flugkapitän Dipl.-Ing Alfred Henke, was requisitioned to fly two Spanish generals, Luis Orgaz and Francisco Franco, to Tetuán, in Spanish Morocco. Here, they joined a clique of discontented right-wing 'rebel' generals who, for some time, had been plotting action against the new, democratically constituted government of the Spanish Republic. D-APOK operated on the DLH air mail 'relay' route from Germany to South America, and at the time was on its way from Bathurst, in The Gambia, via Villa Cisneros in the Spanish Sahara, to Las Palmas. Having arrived at Las Palmas, the Ju 52/3m was effectively impounded by the rebel Spanish military.

After a day or so of uncomfortable exchanges between the local Lufthansa representative and the Spanish, the German aircraft and crew were 'released' and the latter reluctantly agreed to fly a party of Spanish generals and senior officers to Tetuán. After more wrangling and some financial reparations to cover costs, under request from the Spanish, a still unhappy and uncertain Henke flew his Ju 52/3mge to Tablada, near Seville. On the 23rd he left Tablada bound for Germany carrying two expatriate German 'emissaries' of the rebel movement and a Spanish Air Force officer who planned to appeal to Nazi Germany for aid for the still embryonic but growing 'Nationalist' movement.

In the early morning hours of 26 July 1936, Adolf Hitler, buoyed by his enjoyment of a performance of Wagner's opera *Siegfried* at Bayreuth earlier that night, took the momentous decision to offer military support to the Nationalist generals. This had not been a spur-of-the-moment decision, for Hitler was well briefed. There had been nearly 150 years of social unrest and political turbulence in Spain. Hitler knew that there was a prospect of a long civil war there, but also that the rebels' position was tenuous. His ambassador in Madrid had already warned of 'the Bolshevik danger'. A Republican victory in any war in the country would have grave ramifications for German interests, with the unpalatable prospect of a Spanish soviet regime neighbouring France which, in turn, held an alliance with Russia. Furthermore, Hermann Göring had outlined to Hitler the potential longer-term economic benefits to be gained by supporting a victorious Nationalist regime. The nominal leader of the rebels, Gen Franco, had sent a letter asking for rifles, anti-aircraft (AA) guns, fighters and transport aircraft. Hitler made up his mind. Support would be given.

Flugkapitän Henke promptly boarded his Ju 52/3m and flew the emissaries back to Morocco in a ten-hour flight that took them over

Switzerland and the coasts of France, Italy and Spain. To accomplish this, the Junkers had all its surplus equipment removed in favour of a maximum load of fuel. The delegates landed in Morocco on 28 July to be welcomed by anxious Spanish officers who pressed them for details of Hitler's response to their request. They were informed that help was on its way in the form of German military technicians, artillery, ammunition, 20 Ju 52/3m transports and six He 51 fighters.

Beginning in late July, a fleet of Ju 52/3mges flew to Morocco, their immediate task being to airlift Moroccan troops of Franco's *Ejército de Africa* (Army of Africa) to temporary landing grounds at Jerez de la Frontera and Seville, in Spain, in order to bolster the Nationalist military effort in the southern part of the country. These ferry flights were highly dangerous, with the Junkers being laden to capacity with the Moroccans and their weapons and equipment. All seating was removed and the '*Moros*' would sit on the metal floors clutching their rifles and personal packs with their knees drawn up to their chins.

Henke was the first German pilot to commence the flights. As soon as he had landed the German/Spanish delegation in Tetuán, 22 Moroccan soldiers climbed aboard his Ju 52/3m for the journey to Spain. Henke then returned to collect another load – this time more than 30 troops.

Whenever possible, flights were made either in the early morning daylight or during the evening to avoid winds, to conserve fuel and to avoid air sickness among the soldiers in the hot, cramped confines of the heavily laden aircraft. The Junkers usually flew three to four missions per day at altitudes between 2500 and 3500 m in order to evade government ship-mounted AA. Between 29 July and 5 August alone, they carried 1500 men across the Alboran Sea and the Strait of Gibraltar. After the first five days flights to Seville ceased because it was an hour farther on than Jerez; the 40-minute trip meant substantial savings could be made on fuel – the latter was always a problem, as was supply. Water tankers would drive to Tangiers to collect fuel purchased from Portuguese suppliers.

Soon more Junkers arrived, however, flying in to Seville from Dessau via Stuttgart and Rome, although things did not always go according to plan. On one occasion, Junkers pilots had observed the Republican destroyer *Churruca* and the cruiser *Jamie I* in the Bay of Malaga, shortly after which the cruiser opened fire on the German machines as they crossed the water. The warships' defensive fire forced the transports to fly at higher altitudes resulting in their having to take lighter loads. On 8 August, one pilot arriving from Germany landed accidentally at Barajas, Madrid, in Republican-held territory. Fortunately, a Lufthansa crewman flying a Ju 52/3m out of Madrid with German citizens managed to warn the pilot before it was too late and he took off immediately, only to then run low

This was one of the first Ju 52/3ms of the *Legion Condor* to arrive in Spain in 1936. The German officer clad in civilian clothes and the fuel drum lend a sense of scale, particularly in respect to the size of the Junkers' wheel spats

on fuel. He made a forced landing at Azuaga, near the Portuguese border, again in Republican territory. After much wrangling between the German authorities and the Spanish government, which suspected it to be a military machine, the Junkers' crew was sent back to Madrid and from there to Germany, but their aircraft remained at Barajas until it was destroyed in a Nationalist air raid.

Meanwhile, one Luftwaffe bomber pilot who had arrived in Cadiz with the first ten crews, Oberleutnant Rudolf 'Bubb' Freiherr von Moreau, took it upon himself to modify two Junkers to carry 250 kg bombs. In the early morning of 13 August the Ju 52/3ms, flown respectively by Moreau and Henke, flew an attack on the *Jamie I*. Henke's aircraft emerged from cloud, and at 400 m dropped three bombs, two of which hit the ship, the second striking the bridge and severely damaging the vessel. The cruiser had to be taken under tow to Cartagena with nearly 50 dead on board. The *Behelfsbomber* had undergone its true baptism of fire.

Two days later, a Ju 52/3m crashed at Jerez moments after takeoff and two of its crew were killed. Despite this first loss, and as a direct result of Henke's success against the *Jamie I*, four more Ju 52/3ms were converted into bombers at the workshops in Seville. The six *Behelfsbomber* were named *PEDRO 1* to *3* and *PABLO 1* to *3* – tongue-in-cheek references to the names with which Spanish servicemen referred to their German compadres, with 'Bubb' Moreau taking command of the '*PEDRO Kette*' and Oberleutnant Rudolf Joester leading the '*PABLO Kette*'.

In fact, Hitler had sent the Junkers to Franco not only because they were needed to transport troops to the mainland, but also because Franco's position in North Africa was easier to reach than Gen Emilio Mola's *Ejercito Nacional del Norte* (Army of the North). Based at Burgos, Mola's force was suffering from a dire shortage of ammunition, which Franco would be able to replenish once he advanced from the south. By August 1936 Spain was broadly cut in two, with Mola controlling much of the north (except the Basque coastal area and hinterland around Gijon, Santander and Bilbao), while Franco was gaining territory by advancing from the south, and pushing on towards Córdoba. The rest of Spain, bar a few isolated Nationalist strongholds, was Republican.

The Nationalist goal was Madrid, symbolic, but held firmly by the Republic. If Madrid could be taken, the Republican infrastructure would splinter and eventually collapse. To do this, Franco, with his forces now 'on the ground', intended to advance north from Seville to Mérida and connect with Mola, before clearing Badajoz of enemy troops and establishing a link with Portugal, through which supplies would be brought. Following that, the way would be open for an advance on Madrid. Franco's forces duly met up with Mola just north of Mérida, where the badly needed ammunition was handed over, before the advance on Madrid continued eastward along the valley of the Tajo under the overall command of Col Blanco Yagüe.

Nine Junkers were delivered to the Spanish, who used them to equip three *escuadrillas* of three aircraft each. After some hasty training given by the Germans, they too were operational by early August, although on the 10th Capt Francisco Díaz-Trechuelo, commander of the 1ª *Escuadrilla*, was killed by ground fire over the city of Toledo, 70 km south of Madrid. The Junkers was flown back to base by Díaz-Trechuelo's co-pilot, Fernández Matamoros. During a subsequent raid on Don Benito aerodrome the Nationalist Ju 52/3ms were attacked by enemy fighters, and shortly thereafter they were relocated to Cáceres. For the rest of August, re-designated as *Escuadra* B, the unit flew over the Madrid sector, attacking Getafe and Barajas. At the end of the month 1ª *Escuadrilla* moved to Leon, from where it made raids on Irún.

Henke and Moreau continued their missions, and on 23 August for example, despite strong enemy ground fire, they dropped food, medical supplies and mail to 1300 rebel soldiers and 500 women and children besieged in the ancient stone fortress of Alcázar de Toledo, in Toledo. In an intrepid display of flying skill, Moreau carried out a second flight in which he successfully dropped supplies into the 60 m x 70 m inner courtyard of the fortress, despite heavy ground fire that riddled his aircraft. The next day, Ju 52/3ms attacked the Republican airfield at Getafe under escort from Spanish-flown He 51s.

On the transport side, by the end of August, 20 Ju 52/3ms had ferried 10,500 troops, and during the following month a further 9700 were flown across. Furthermore, 36,867 kg of supplies were brought in during the first week of September. By 11 October, 13,523 men and just over 270,000 kg of equipment and supplies, including 36 artillery pieces and 127 machine guns, had been ferried to the Spanish mainland. On one day Alfred Henke took no fewer than 241 *Moros*. In 1942, harking back to this operation, Hitler commented famously, 'Franco ought to erect a monument to the glory of the Junkers 52'. Certainly, it was the first time in military aeronautics that such an airlift had been attempted – and with such success.

The first Ju 52/3m to be lost in aerial combat was the Spanish 2ª *Escuadrilla*'s 22-64, which was shot down by a Republican fighter over Toledo on 28 September. The crew was killed.

Meanwhile, acting on the *Führer*'s instructions, Erhard Milch, now a *General der Flieger* and Secretary of State for Aviation, and other senior

Three Spanish-crewed Ju 52/3ms of the 3ª *Escuadrilla* 'Tres Marias', *Grupo de Bombardeo Nocturno* 2-E-22 in close formation over Spain in late 1936/early 1937. Seen here are 22•61 *MARIA DE LA O'* and 22•62 *MARIA MAGDALENA*, which also carried the name *TRECHUELO* beneath the cockpit after Francisco Díaz-Trechuelo, the first leader of 1ª *Escuadrilla* who was killed by ground fire in August 1936. Clearly visible is the dorsal gunner in 22•61 manning his MG 15 machine gun. Note the small and probably very inadequate gunner's windshield

Bombs lie in the open on a typical forward airfield in Spain, with a Ju 52/3m of K/88 forming a backdrop

figures moved quickly, and within days a military force of men, tanks, guns and aircraft was being assembled in Germany. To the outside world, this would be a 'volunteer' force. By early August the first German airmen were in Spain, and by the autumn, under the watchful eye of Göring, German aid to Nationalist Spain expanded and accelerated. Eventually, following the failure of Franco's attempt to take Madrid and the influx of Soviet war *matériel* to the Republican cause, the Nazis decided to intervene on a more entrenched and committed scale in the Spanish Civil War. On 7 November, as a consequence of these developments, it was decided to form a 'legion' with which to fight the threat of internationalised Bolshevism. To the world this legion would be seen as embarking on a crusade against the dark forces of oppression. Hence was born the *Legion Condor*.

An order of battle for the air component was drawn up which saw the establishment of a fighter *Gruppe* (J/88), a bomber *Gruppe* (K/88), reconnaissance and maritime reconnaissance *Gruppen* (A/88 and AS/88), a flak detachment (F/88) plus a signals/communications group and maintenance, hospital, supply, salvage, testing and experimental, meteorological and liaison elements. Ten Ju 52/3ms were delivered to Dessau and the Junkers workforce was ordered to strip out all military equipment from the aircraft and cover their gun mountings with metal sheet. The aircraft were then painted with civil codes. Within 24 hours the Ju 52/3ms were packed into large, unmarked wooden crates and delivered to Hamburg docks for shipment on a fleet of freighters.

By the end of October, there was a total of 28 Ju 52/3ms in Spain attached to K/88. 1.K/88 under Oberleutnant Heinz Liegnitz was at Salamanca/San Fernando alongside 2.K/88 under Hauptmann Anselm Brasser, while 3.K/88 under Hauptmann Krafft von Dellmensingen was based initially at Seville, before it joined with the other *Staffeln*.

By 29 November 1936, thousands of men, hundreds of tanks, guns, aircraft, weapons and many tons of equipment had been shipped to Spain. Earlier that month the Nationalists had launched their drive on Madrid. The Republicans fought desperately to defend the capital, but the government was eventually forced to evacuate to Valencia. By 4 November the Nationalists had taken the airport at Getafe, and, by the 6th, although outnumbered with just over 12,000 men supported by a handful of armoured cars and light tanks, they had reached the outskirts of the capital. Its one million inhabitants had been mobilised and fortified with extreme Communist propaganda to defend the city at all costs. Indeed, women had been ordered to pour burning oil on the enemy if necessary.

Ju 52/3ms, escorted by *Legion Condor* He 51s, initially undertook attacks on Madrid from airfields in the Salamanca area. They encountered little opposition and were able to operate virtually without hindrance. Missions were also flown to Malaga, Cartagena, Almeria, Alicante, Valencia and Oviedo, where the Junkers provided support to isolated Nationalist forces by bombing enemy positions, as well as dropping in badly needed food and weapons. These missions involved long approach routes and, on occasion, temporary transfer to another airfield closer to the target, and they placed considerable strain on the ground personnel and servicing infrastructure. As a measure of how slender resources were, however, operations against Malaga harbour were carried out by just two Ju 52/3ms and a pair of Hs 123s escorted by Italian CR.32s.

On 4 November, a Ju 52/3m piloted by Leutnant Kolbitz was lost as a result of the first encounter with a Russian-supplied Polikarpov I-15, a highly manoeuvrable biplane fighter armed with four PV-1 7.62 mm machine guns. A Spanish-flown Junkers from *Escuadra* B was badly damaged in a similar attack, the aeroplane being forced to land at Esquivias with a fatally wounded observer on board.

By November *Escuadra* B was formed of 1ª *Escuadrilla* 'Sanjurjo' under Capt Mendizábal, 2ª *Escuadrilla* 'Toledo' under Capt Carrillo, 3ª *Escuadrilla* 'Les Tres Marías' under Capt Guerero, all named after the heroines of popular songs, and 4ª *Escuadrilla* led by Capt Pardo. The 1ª and 4ª *Escuadrilla* were subsequently combined to form the *Grupo de Bombardeo Nocturno*

Five Italian-manned Ju 52/3ms take off for another bombing raid over Republican lines. Curiously, the aircraft at the head of the *Kette* and the machine to its left carry incomplete Nationalist rudder markings

A formation of eight Ju 52/3ms pass low over a Spanish town. As supplies of new Soviet-supplied fighters bolstered the strength of the Republican air force, such unescorted and slow formations became increasingly vulnerable to attack

(night-bombing group), the *Escuadrilla* being redesignated 1-E-22 and 2-E-22, respectively. The 2ª and 3ª *Escuadrilla* were re-designated 3-E-22 and 4-E-22. Additionally, some of the first German Ju 52/3ms sent to Spain were delivered to the Nationalists, who used them to establish two further units, the 5-E-22 'Barbarán' and 6-E-22 'Navarra'.

On 17 November, aircraft from 3-E-22 and the *Grupo de Bombardeo Nocturno* struck at the Florida and del Rey bridges in Madrid as well as key streets believed to be the location of Republican commanders, stores and communications hubs. But it was becoming a tough war – six Ju 52/3ms of 3-E-22 and 4-E-22 were damaged in an air raid on Navalmoral airfield on 4 December. The airframes were dismantled and moved to Tablada for repair, keeping them out of frontline service for two months.

German raids on the Spanish capital, as well as against Republican-held airfields located around it, continued in December despite atrocious weather and, on occasion, 40 tons of bombs were dropped at a time. By working with ground forces, tactically, the raids were timed to arrive just ahead of Nationalist infantry attacks, with the Ju 52/3ms sometimes making diving attacks against airfield targets while German and Italian escort fighters carried out simultaneous strafing runs. On the 13th, a *Kette* from K/88 led by Oberleutnant von Nordeck took off from Salamanca on a long-range mission for Cordoba, where they were each bombed up with 20 50 kg bombs to attack a target in the Bujalance area to the west of Cordoba. One aircraft was reported to have been shot down during the operation, but it later transpired it had flown into a mountain at Gredos.

With the arrival of more Soviet and French aircraft in Spain, the Republican air arm was able to bolster its strength – these assets were deployed with priority against the Ju 52/3m raids. It was not uncommon for between 20 and 25 fighters to be in the air at once, including I-15s and the new Polikarpov I-16 '*Mosca*' all-metal, low-wing monoplane fighter, which was dubbed the '*Rata*' by the Germans. The I-16 was fast, and armed with two rapid-firing, wing-mounted 7.62 mm ShKAS machine guns (which packed a greater punch than the weapons fitted to the I-15), it was considered to be the best fighter in the world at that point.

On one occasion a Ju 52/3m was so badly hit by fire from an I-16 that its pilot made a forced landing. The German formation commander, von Moreau, duly took it upon himself to land his own Junkers close to the landing site, which was on a rough, exposed, hillside and which he believed to be in enemy territory, in order to rescue his comrades. It transpired that the Junkers had actually come down only 100 m behind Nationalist lines, but notwithstanding that, in a demonstration of the ruggedness of the Ju 52/3m, von Moreau took off with the shot-down crew on board and returned safely to Salamanca.

On 5 December a Lufthansa Ju 52/3m was posted missing whilst on a flight from Salamanca to Berlin, and three days later Oberleutnant Liegnitz, the *Staffelkapitän* of 1.K/88, was reported as having been shot down and his gunner wounded in the head.

On 15 January 1937, following meticulous planning involving Nationalist ground forces as well as several reconnaissance flights, a formation of 34 Ju 52/3ms set out from Salamanca to bomb the port at Cartagena, a target that Spanish-flown Junkers had already made attacks against three months earlier. The raid was led by no less a figure than Generalmajor Hugo Sperrle, the commander of the *Legion Condor*. As a first leg, the bomb-laden Junkers made for Morocco, to where some 40 tons of fuel, together with equipment and ground personnel had been shipped in advance of the raid from Cadiz. Despite the prospect of making hazardous landings with bombs on board, all aircraft came down safely. After refuelling and a quick mechanical check, the Ju 52/3ms took off in pairs at ten-minute intervals bound for Cartagena.

Three *Ketten* of Ju 52/3ms rumble over the cameraman somewhere in northern Spain

Reaching the port in the late afternoon, the Junkers left buildings and at least two ships on fire, while other vessels were forced to steam away. The port itself was left heavily damaged and out of commission. The bombers then returned to Africa, and the following day flew back to Salamanca. There was to be no respite, however, for that evening they were detailed to bomb Madrid again. The *Behelfsbomber* had proved itself.

Indeed, as the battlefronts of the Spanish Civil War ebbed and flowed throughout 1936 and 1937, so there was, in the absence of a sufficient quantity and mobility of Nationalist artillery and armour, a tendency for air support to be called upon as flying artillery. During the opening months of the war, Oberstleutnant Dr.-Ing. Wolfram Freiherr von Richthofen, who would go on to become Chief of Staff and eventually commander of the *Legion Condor*, devised methods of coordination between air and ground forces – no easy task when it meant striving for cooperation between Spanish, German and Italian commanders.

Initially, von Richthofen directed the Junkers against targets in the enemy rear such as harbours, road junctions, storage facilities and ammunition dumps. Then, from the spring of 1937, following the launch of a Nationalist offensive in the north, missions against Bilbao, Santander and Gijon took on much more of a tactical nature, with the Ju 52/3ms being deployed directly over the frontline, operating at the request of, and in support of, the ground forces. These operations would be followed by attacks against any remaining centres of Republican resistance, reserves, and assembly areas, with several such missions being flown in one day.

The skill and capabilities of the crews, who were largely inexperienced in lower level, landmark navigation, were frequently stretched to the limit as they searched for small, mobile targets often set against difficult terrain in bad weather whilst navigating their way over the high mountains of Spain. In order for the Ju 52/3ms to reach Madrid from their bases around Salamanca the Junkers had to cross the Sierra de Guadarrama – a range of mountains which not only formed a natural barrier, but which was also subject to changes in weather (*text continues on page 48*)

COLOUR PLATES

1
Ju 52/3m Wk-Nr 4009 CB-18 *HUANUNI* of the *Fuerza Aérea Boliviana*, Bolivia, 1933

2
Ju 52/3m Wk-Nr 5020 D-AZIS *HORST WESSEL* of the *Regierungsstaffel*, 1935

34

3
Ju 52/3m 27+E11 of 1./KG 753, Gotha, late 1935

4
Ju 52/3mg3e S7+L15 of *Fliegergruppe (S)* or *Grosse Kampffliegerschule Lechfeld*, Lechfeld, 1935-38

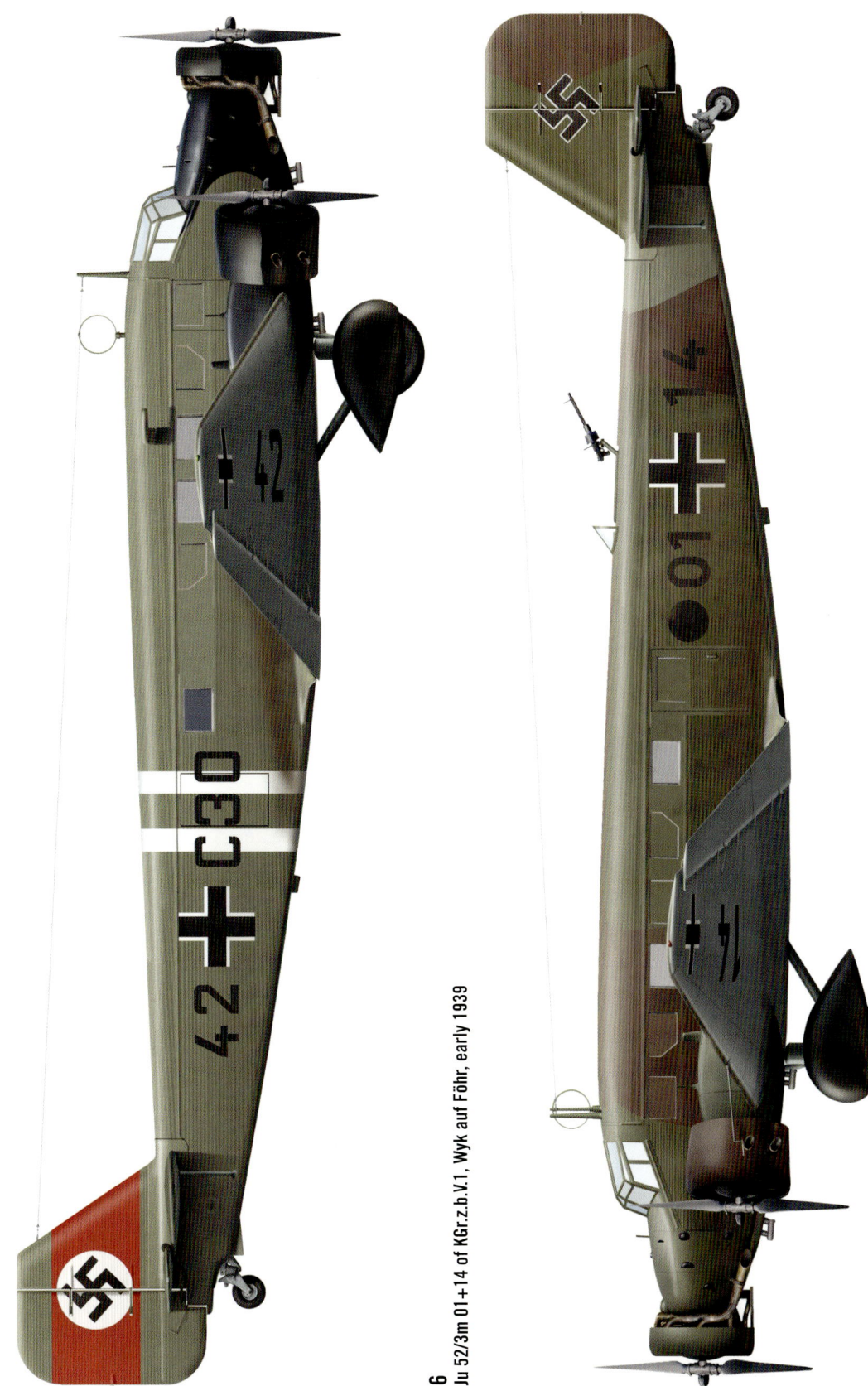

5 Ju 52/3m 42+C30 of II./KG 254, Eschwege or Giessen, 1937

6 Ju 52/3m 01+14 of KGr.z.b.V.1, Wyk auf Föhr, early 1939

7
Ju 52/3m 21+H12 of 2./KG 152, Neubrandenburg, 1937

8
Ju 52/3mg3e 22•73 *PEDRO 3* of 3.K/88, *Legion Condor*, Spain, 1937

37

9
Ju 52/3mg3e 22•61 *MARIA DE LA O*' of 3. *Escuadrilla* 'Tres Marias', *Grupo de Bombardeo Nocturno* 2-E-22, Spain, 1937

10
Ju 52/3mg3e 22•90 of 2.K/88, *Legion Condor*, possibly Sabadell, Spain, 1937-38

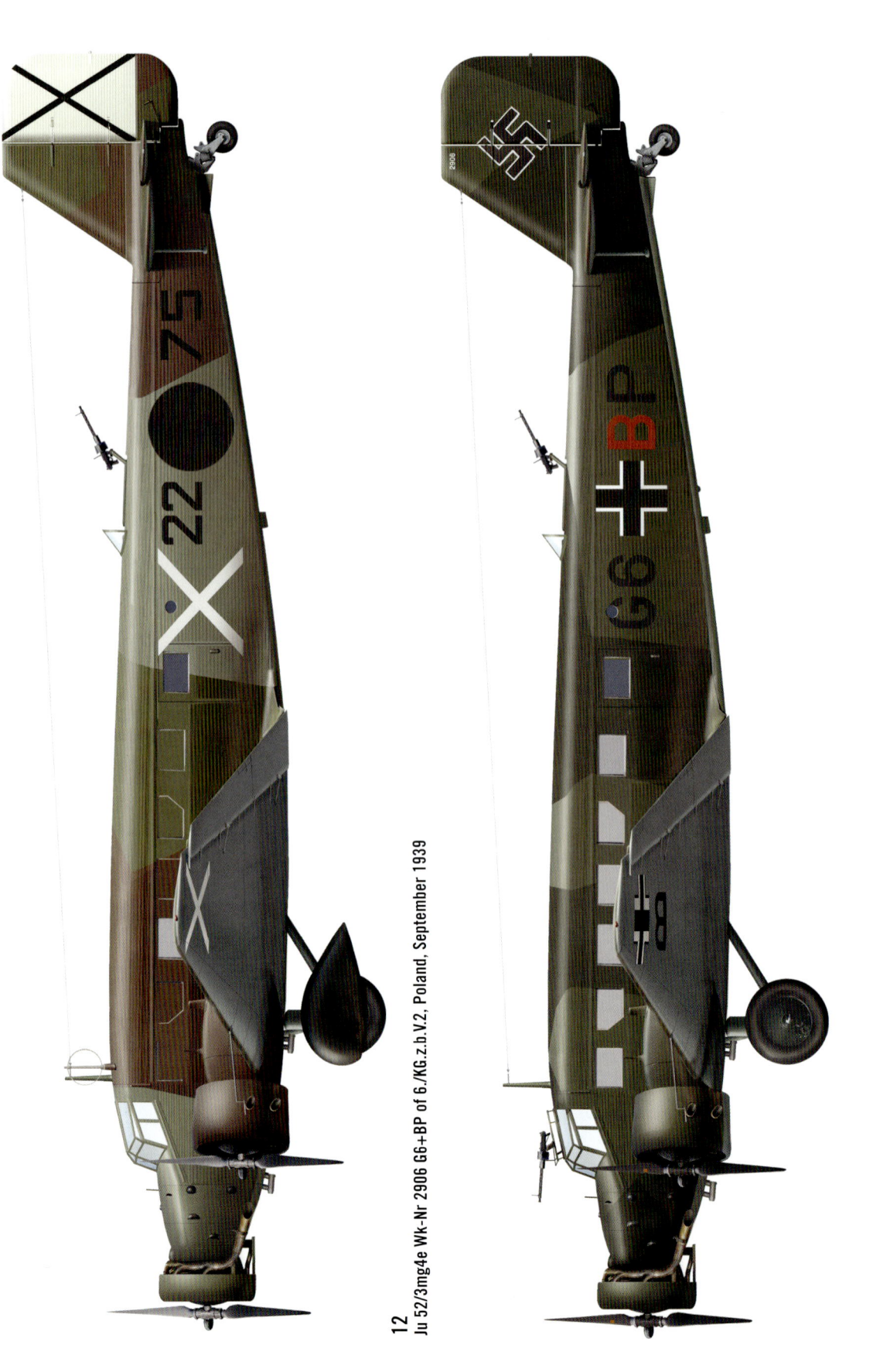

11
Ju 52/3mg3e 22•75 of 3.K/88, *Legion Condor*, Seville, Spain, 1939

12
Ju 52/3mg4e Wk-Nr 2906 G6+BP of 6./KG.z.b.V.2, Poland, September 1939

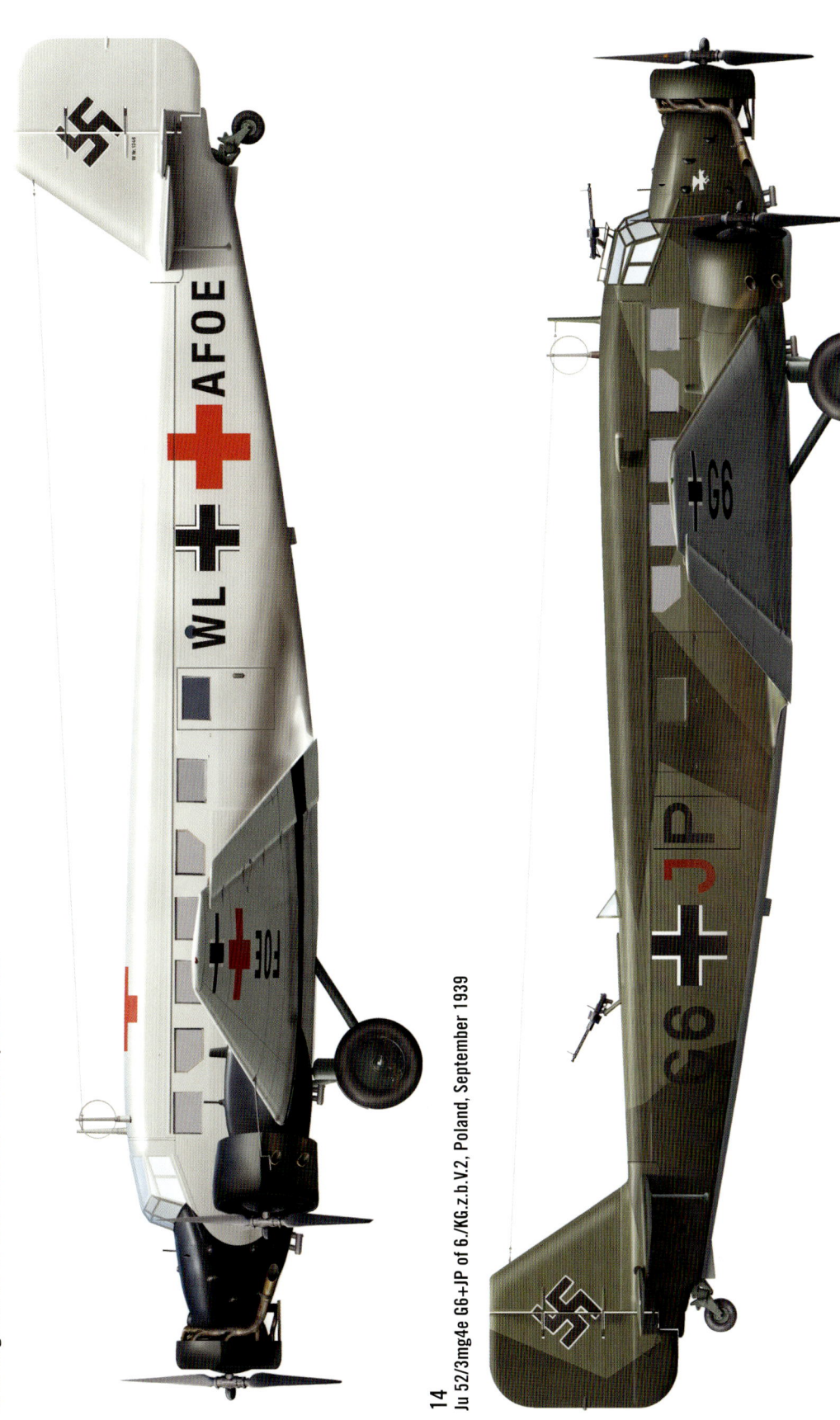

13
Ju 52/3mg4e(S) Wk-Nr 1348 WL+AFOE, Poland, September 1939

14
Ju 52/3mg4e G6+JP of 6./KG.z.b.V.2, Poland, September 1939

40

15
Ju 52/3mg4e 1Z+GW of 12./KG.z.b.V.1, Poland, September 1939

16
Ju 52/3mg4e Wk-Nr 6821 VB+UP of KGr.z.b.V.102, Norway, April 1940

17
Ju 52/3mg4e 1Z+LM of 4./KG.z.b.V.1, Norway, April 1940

18
Ju 52/3mg4e 1Z+BN of 5./KG.z.b.V.1, Germany, April 1940

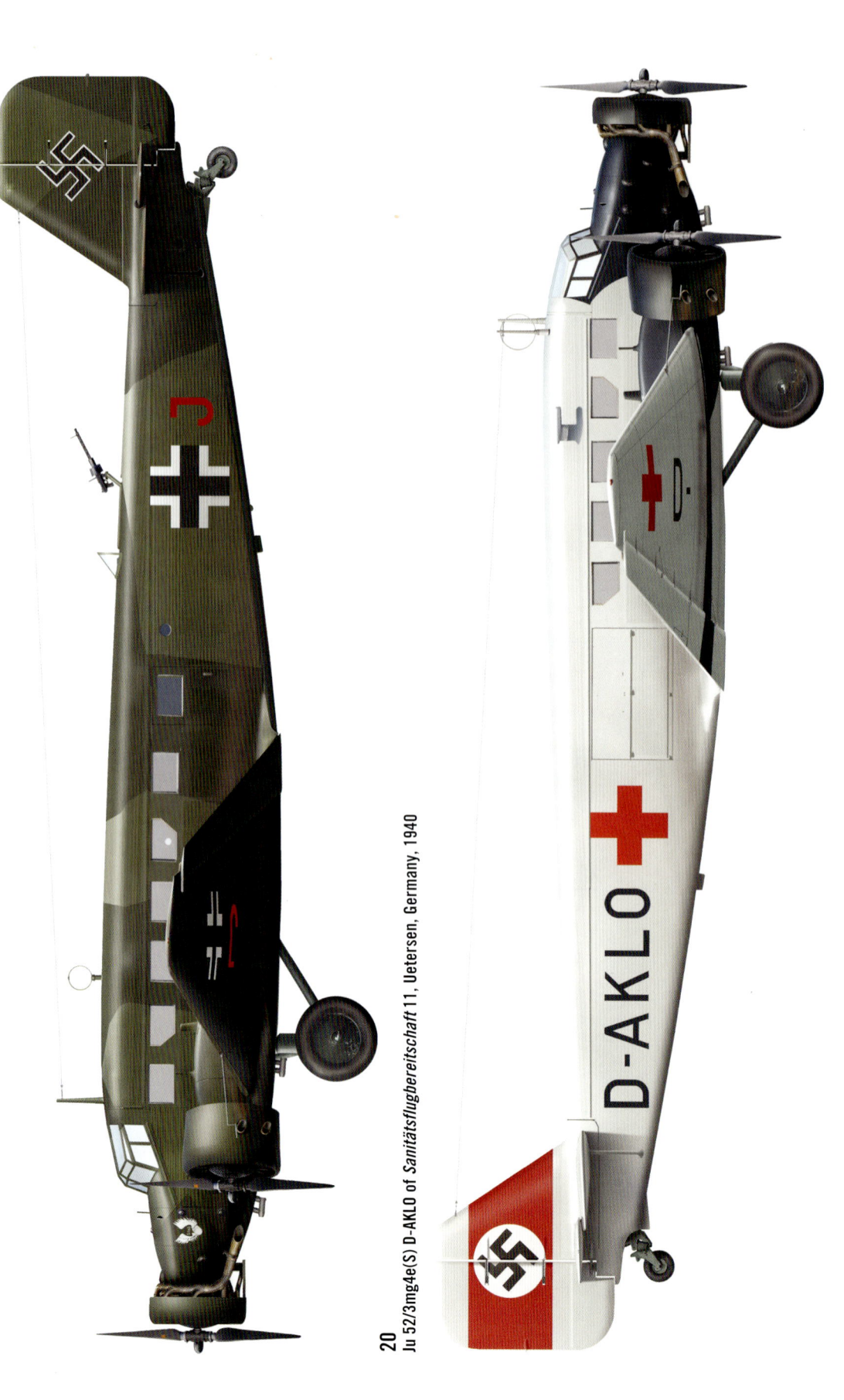

19
Ju 52/3mg4e 'J' of Stab/KGr.z.b.V.108, Norway, April 1940

20
Ju 52/3mg4e(S) D-AKLO of Sanitätsflugbereitschaft 11, Uetersen, Germany, 1940

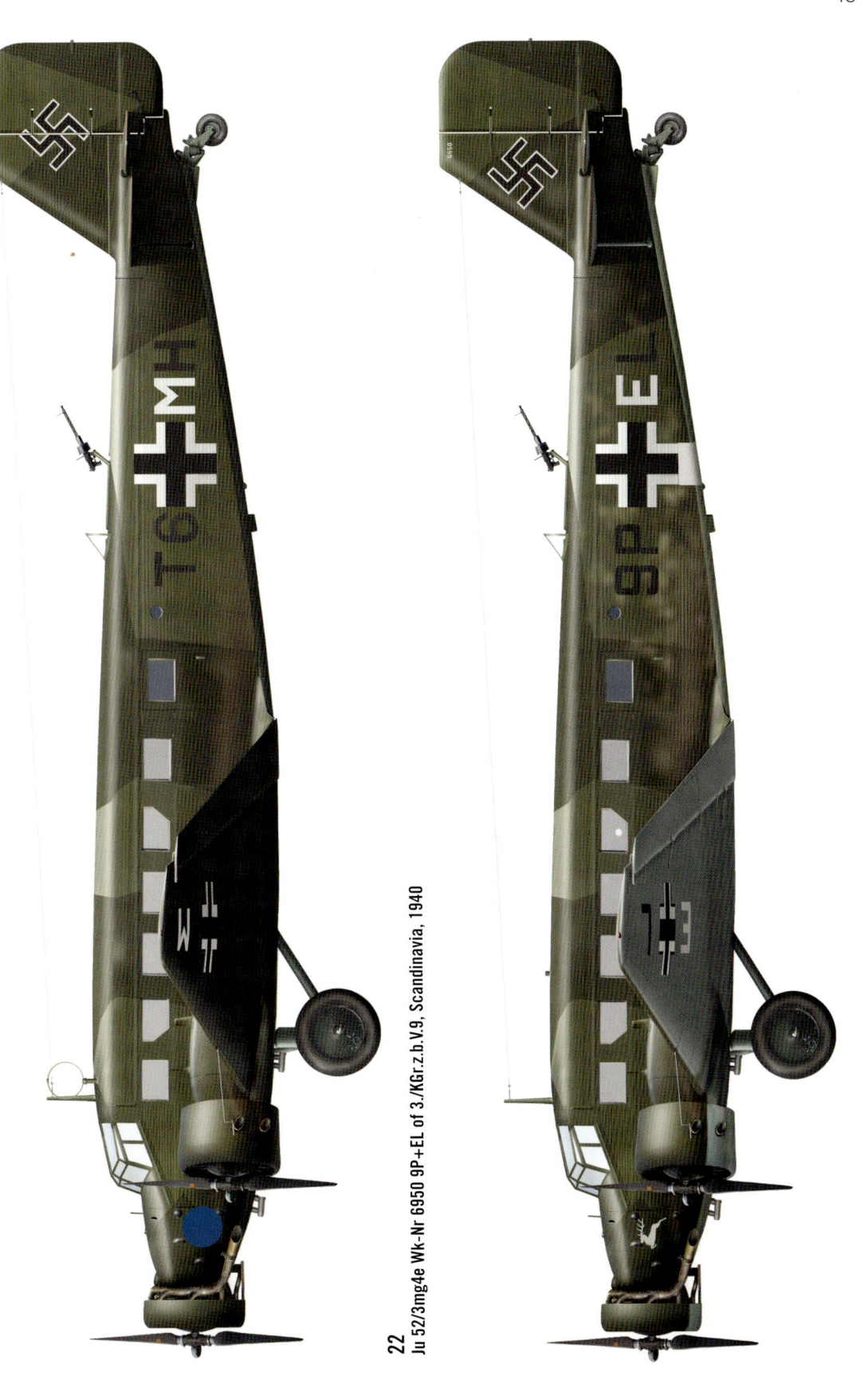

21
Ju 52/3mg4e T6+MH of 1./*Sturzkampfgeschwader* 2 'Immelmann', Germany, April 1940

22
Ju 52/3mg4e Wk-Nr 6950 9P+EL of 3./KGr.z.b.V.9, Scandinavia, 1940

44

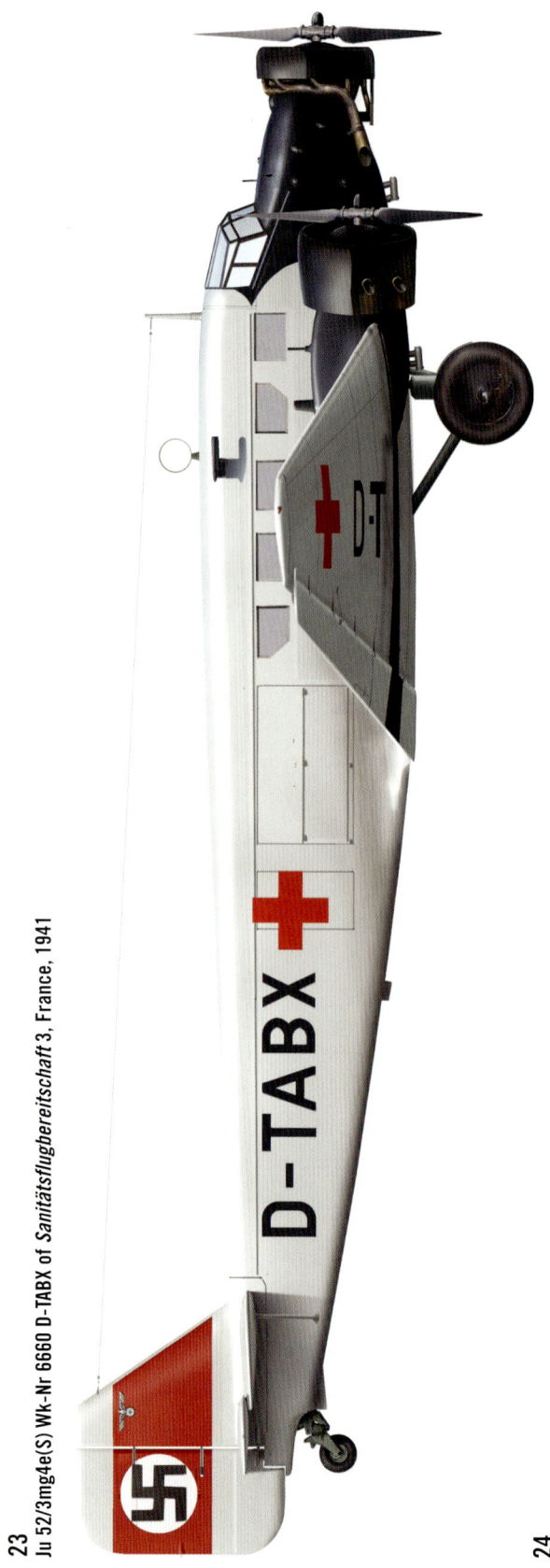

23
Ju 52/3mg4e(S) Wk-Nr 6660 D-TABX of *Sanitätsflugbereitschaft* 3, France, 1941

24
Ju 52/3mg4e 5K+VN of II./KG 3, Antwerp-Duerne or Bremen, 1940

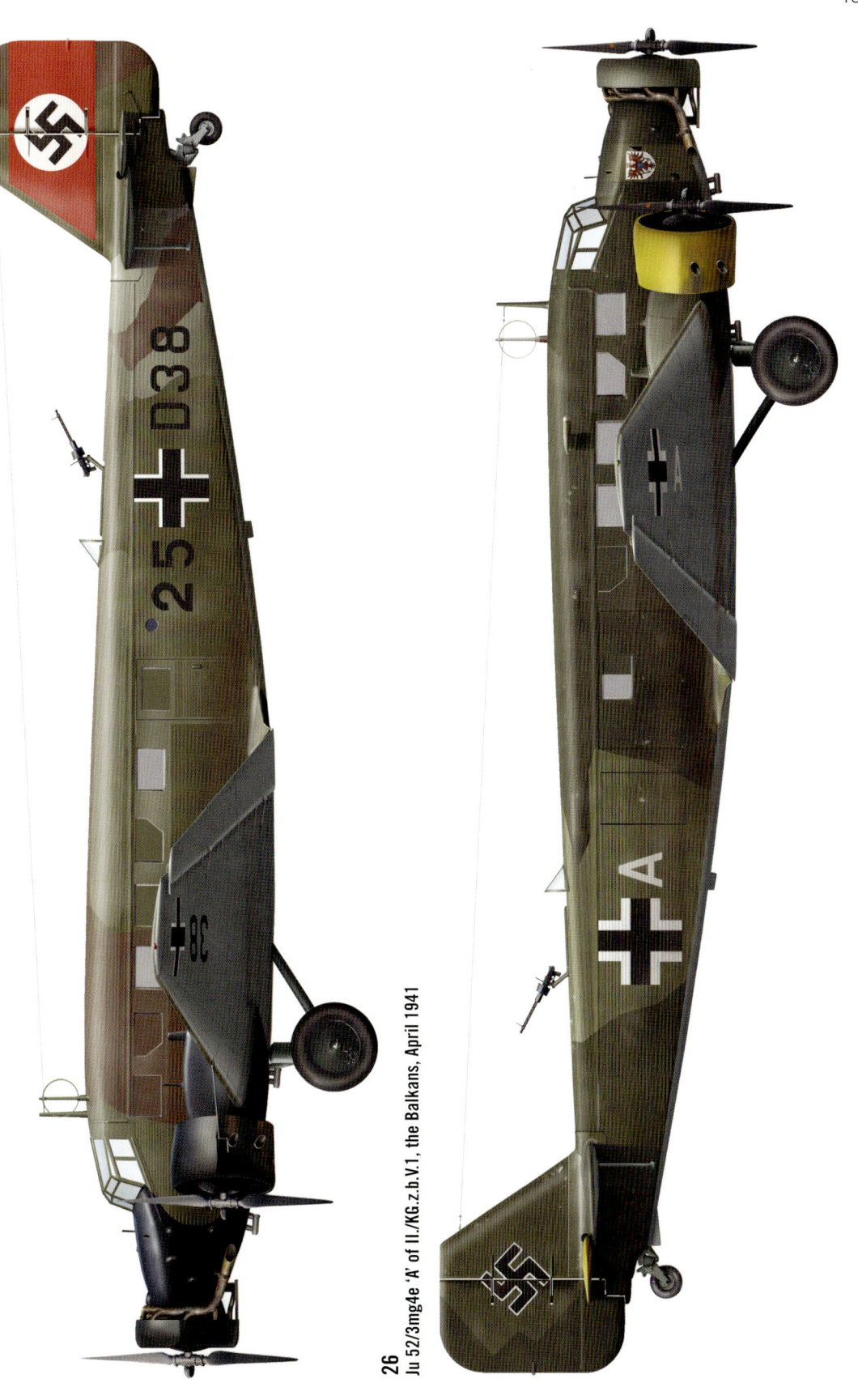

25
Ju 52/3mg4e 25+D38 of III./KG.z.b.V.1, possibly Stendal, spring 1940

26
Ju 52/3mg4e 'A' of II./KG.z.b.V.1, the Balkans, April 1941

46

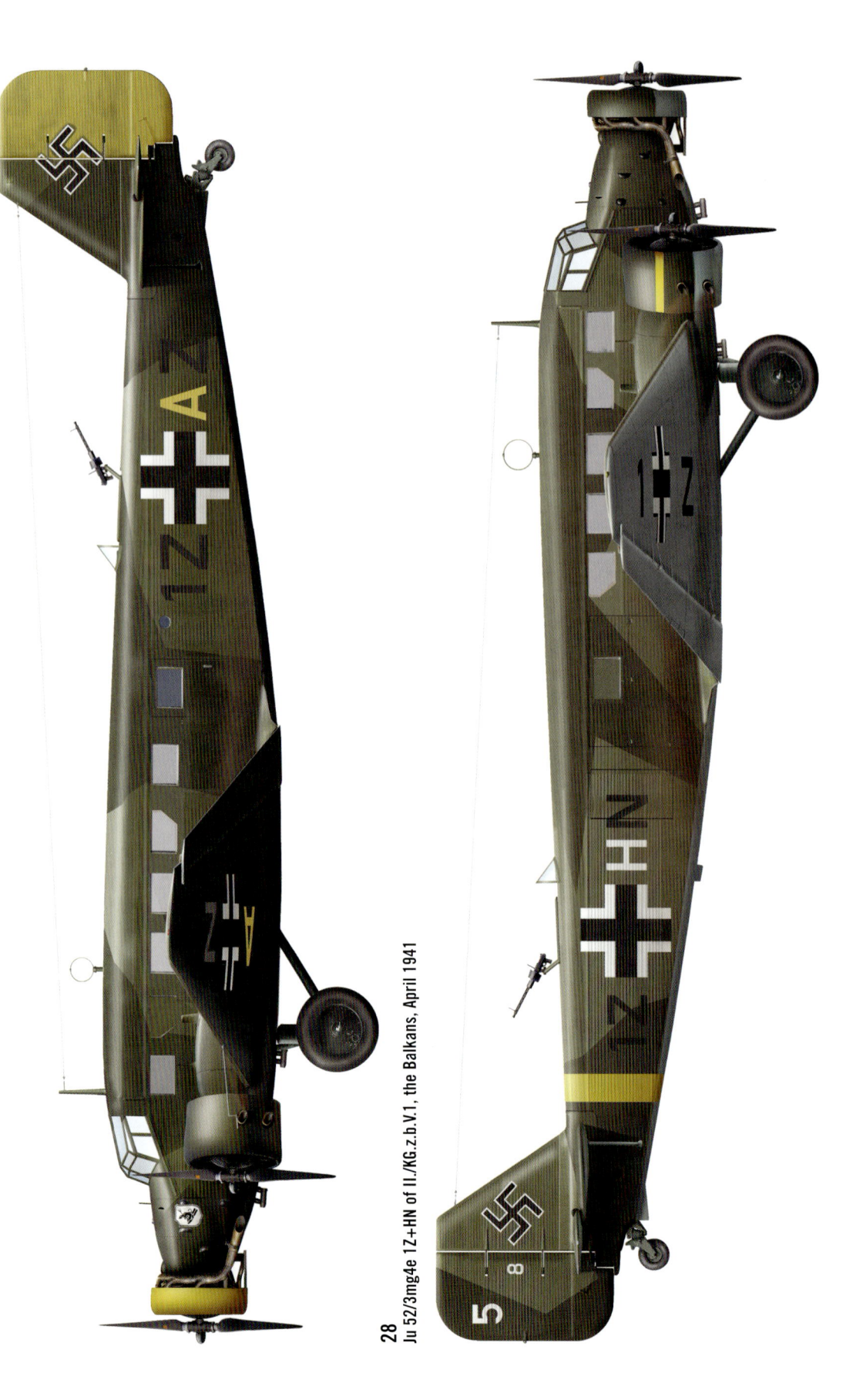

27
Ju 52/3mg4e 1Z+AZ of IV./KG.z.b.V.1, the Balkans, April 1941

28
Ju 52/3mg4e 1Z+HN of II./KG.z.b.V.1, the Balkans, April 1941

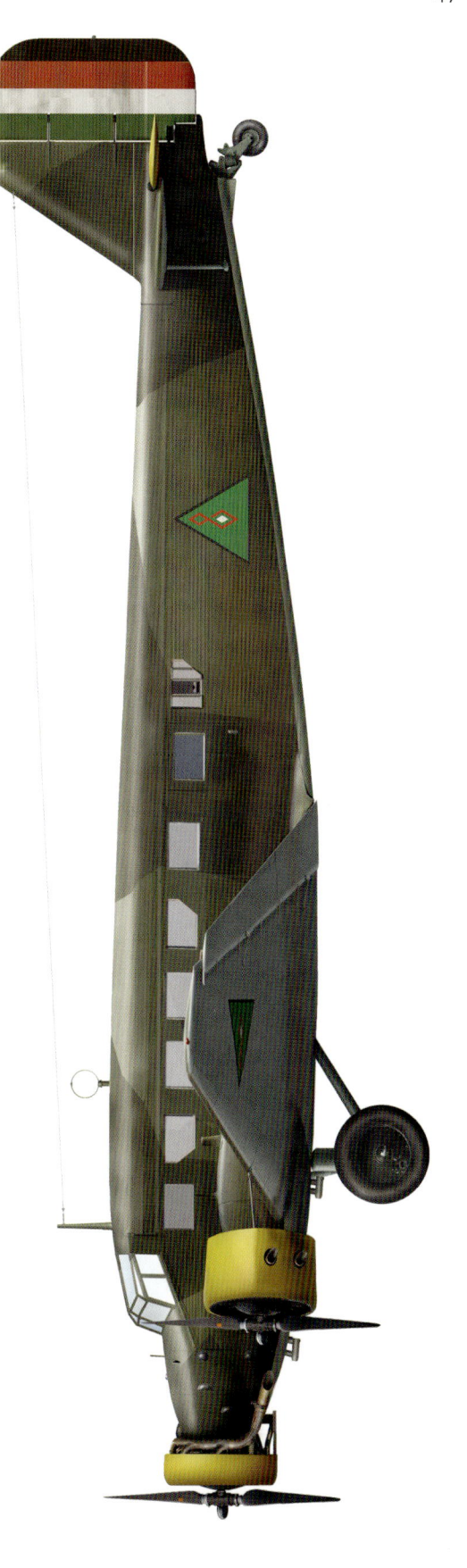

29
Ju 52/3mg4e G6+DX of KGr.z.b.V.105, Greece, May 1941

30
Ju 52/3mg4e of *Sonderkommando Junck*, Mosul, Iraq, May 1941

on its slopes. In cold temperatures, the Junkers lacked the capability to overfly them because of the risk of icing. The shifting nature of the war in Spain at this time also meant that detailed planning and information on targets was often lacking, with targets sometimes changing at a moment's notice. Crews also had to cope with a lack of radio communication equipment, the aeroplane's paucity of power in the climb and its inadequate combat manoeuvrability.

Depending on the target, the Ju 52/3ms would adopt different formations, flying tight and close in cases where bombs had to cover a small area, or in a more dispersed manner when operating against larger or multiple targets. In such instances the Junkers would split up into groups of six, with each group assigned its own specific target within the overall targets. Being solely responsible for the destruction of its assigned target, a group would, on occasion, return to a target to ensure the successful completion of its mission. However, it was vital that the bombers retained their formation during their approach to the target, over the target and on their return, since success depended on formational defence in order to ensure minimal losses.

The maximum bomb load for a Ju 52/3m in Spain was 1500 kg of high-explosive and/or incendiary bombs, but because of the relatively primitive condition of the airfields, with frequently soft or uneven ground, combined with the quantity of fuel needed for long-range missions, it was quite usual for bomb-loads to have to be reduced to 1000-1200 kg. Bombing effectiveness relied more on the skills and experience of the crews rather than on the bomb-aiming equipment, which had been designed for higher-altitude missions and straight and level approaches. The maximum fuel load of 1875 litres was sufficient for five hours' flying and, assuming average fuel consumption of 375 litres per hour, this meant a combat speed of approximately 210 km/h at an altitude of 3000 m. Thus with a bomb load of 1000 kg, the Ju 52/3mge had a radius of action of around 500 km from its point of departure.

Eventually, however, operations by the comparatively slow and low-flying Ju 52/3ms in strength against well-defended targets in the Republican hinterland became unviable and were mostly discontinued. To a great extent this situation was brought about by the absence of effective fighter escort. The pilots of the *Legion Condor*'s He 51 biplane fighters, of which there were relatively few during the first two years of the war, were not trained in escort or rendezvous techniques. Communications between fighters and bombers were poor and the Ju 52/3ms were just too slow for the Heinkels to remain in formation with, even when the bombers were routed over the fighters' airfield. Despite these difficulties, J/88 always attempted to provide cover when conditions allowed, and, on

Ju 52/3m 22•75 of 3.K/88, with 22•99 of 1.K/88 behind it, in a hangar at Seville for maintenance. The cowl panels have been removed from the engines, as has the windshield and gun mount for the dorsal gun position. The aircraft may have been slated as a source of parts for newer machines

Ju 52/3mg3e 22•48 *NAVARRA* of the 2 *Grupo de Bombardeo Nocturno* (2-G-22) 'Navarra' in 1939

the occasions when targets were close to the front, the fighters remained with the bombers during the actual bombardment. Over Madrid, however, I-15s and I-16s had little difficulty in penetrating the He 51 escort to get at the Ju 52/3ms. Trials at increasing the Junkers' armament to five machine guns (a forward turret, two waist guns and two inner wing-mounted forward-firing guns) achieved little and were not pursued.

As early as February 1937, German and Spanish crews undertook night-bombing raids. On the 15th of that month, 11 Spanish Ju 52/3ms targeted Republican positions at Arganda del Rey, but the acting commander of 3-E-22, Capt José Calderón Gaztelu, was killed by enemy fighters, as were his co-pilot and gunner. The night raids were experimental, relying on the availability of emergency landing grounds and sufficient airfield lighting, though the latter was rarely present. Eventually, blinker lights and directional searchlights were employed to aid navigation and target location, and to mark out key waypoints to and from a target. Occasionally, scout aircraft would drop incendiary bombs as illumination over a target. During night raids, if an escort was provided, it was usually by Italian or Spanish fighters.

In March 1937, mainly as a result of a stall in movement on the Madrid front, most of the *Legion Condor* was transferred to Burgos in readiness for the great Nationalist offensive in the north. The Nationalist objective was the strip of Basque territory along the northern Spanish coast between Gijon and Bilbao and the valuable industrial and mining regions of Vizcaya and Asturias. It would be a campaign fought in bad weather and in difficult terrain.

K/88's serviceable number of Ju 52/3ms had dwindled to just 16, and anticipation was growing over the much-vaunted new He 111B-1s, Do 17s and Ju 86s that were arriving at Seville. However, by 31 March serviceability had evidently improved since 20 Ju 52/3ms attacked Republican lines around the town of Ochandiano, as well as road and rail junctions at Durango, to soften them up in preparation for the main ground assault. On 6 April Ju 52/3ms bombed Bodegas Altún in cloudy weather to make a clear path for Nationalist infantry. Then on 26 April, after weeks of heavy fighting, the *Legion Condor* bombed the Basque town of Guernica as part of its ongoing operations to support the advance northwards. Its actions sent shockwaves rippling through the world's media.

The Nationalists had identified Guernica as a choke point and road intersection through which Republican forces would pass in order to reach safer territory. In doing so, they would cross a bridge at Rentaria.

But first they would have to pass through Guerricaiz, nine kilometres away, and here von Richthofen, by this stage the *Legion*'s Chief of Staff, realised that his bombers could annihilate the Republicans. By destroying the Rentaria bridge the defenders would be contained on the wrong side of the Oca River. But that morning reconnaissance aircraft from A/88 erroneously reported large enemy forces around Guernica. In fact they were civilians on their way to their usual market. Von Richthofen saw a tactical opportunity to use air power to isolate and destroy these 'reserves' and obtained permission from Spanish commanders to attack this new target. Together with the Italians, the *Legion*'s bombers were to strike what were assumed to be 23 battalions of Basque troops on the roads immediately east of Guernica and on its outskirts, as well as against the Rentaria bridge, while J/88 with A/88 would strafe the roads east of the river to force the defenders into Guerricaiz.

However, communications between von Richthofen's command post and the Nationalist HQ at Burgos seem to have failed, ending in confusion, and an attack was ordered on Guernica itself. K/88 and VB/88 duly despatched 26 bombers, escorted by 16 fighters from J/88. Of the bombers, 23 were Ju 52/3ms loaded with 250 kg high-explosive (HE) bombs and 1 kg incendiaries in containers. There would have been two more aircraft had they not been undergoing repairs at Seville. The Junkers approached the town from south to north, following the He 111s and Do 17s of VB/88. Bombs struck the bridge, the centre and south of the town, while a burning olive oil plant caused dense clouds of smoke, confusing later waves of aircraft.

Between 250 and 1500 people were reported as killed or wounded during the bombing attacks – the true number will never be known, and some were strafed by fighters as they tried to escape the carnage. The bridge remained largely unscathed and the bombs missed the assigned targets except for the railway station. A small-arms factory remained untouched, as did the town's two hospitals. On the 30th, von Richthofen visited the town and recorded, 'Guernica, a town of 5000 inhabitants, has been literally razed to the ground. When the first Ju's arrived, there was already smoke to be seen everywhere'. The damage inflicted on Guernica was enough to appal international opinion, and the town held the ignoble distinction of being the first to suffer from a modern 'terror raid'.

On 16 May the whole of K/88 bombed enemy positions around Amorebieta-Etxano, while on 21 and 29 May a force of 21 Ju 52/3ms, along with aircraft from VB/88, bombed the town and enemy positions at Pico de Gorbea.

After Guernica, K/88 continued to fly missions around Brunete, where the first attempt at a large-scale raid by Ju 52/3ms was mounted by K/88 and aircraft of A/88 on 8 July 1937 under escort from the newly arrived Messerschmitt Bf 109s. In missions over two days, the aircraft of K/88 dropped 20,204 kg of incendiaries, as well as 10-, 50- and 250-kg HE bombs.

On 7 July the *Legion Condor* recorded a total of 59 Ju 52/3ms on strength at Salamanca. In the evening of the 16th, K/88, along with aircraft from VB/88, A/88 and Italian Savoias, escorted by CR.32s, He 51s and Bf 109s, carried out a major attack on the Republican breakthrough at Brunete. One German pilot observed how 'heavy bombers – Ju 52s – were deployed in order to plaster particular enemy positions with bombs. The positions were very difficult to make out from the air, hence the bombers had to fly as low as possible and, in addition, had to remain undetected by the AA defences in order to be able to carry out their task'.

With the defeat of the Republican offensive at Brunete and the return of some stability to the Madrid sector, the Nationalists were able to resume operations in the north aimed at capturing what remained of Republican territory in the coastal region west of Bilbao. The target was the port of Santander, followed by an advance into Asturias and the relief of Oviedo.

By early August 1937 K/88 had 18 Ju 52/3ms on strength, and throughout the month the Junkers struck regularly, along with Spanish-crewed machines, around Valmaseda, Cotejon, Solcedillo, Torrebredo and Reinosa. On 23 August, K/88 commenced missions against Asturia and the regional capital, Gijon, including night raids. In September K/88's focus was on the ports of Gijon and Aviles, as well as transport lines behind the enemy front and fortified positions, one of which near Llanes surrendered as a result of the bombing. However, on the 21st a Ju 52/3m of K/88 crashed and exploded on Mount Reinosa and its crew were killed. Three days later the aircraft of Leutnant Ernst König developed technical problems while in a formation out to bomb the Llanes area, and in trying to make an emergency landing in the Pontejos area, they were killed. Then, on 7 October, the Ju 52/3m of Leutnant Heinrich Stallamann was hit by AA fire over Gijon. The crew was observed baling out over enemy territory. It transpired that all were killed except the pilot, Feldwebel Ogaza.

By late November 1937, however, K/88 Ju 52/3m force had dwindled because of its re-equipment with He 111s. The Junkers flew some more night missions before the majority of them was handed over to the Spanish, with one being assigned to each of the major *Legion* units as a transport and communications aircraft. The Spanish continued to fly their Ju 52/3ms on regular missions. On 23 December 1938, the Nationalists listed 23 Junkers on strength, 13 of them at Pallaruelo, four at Sanjurjo, three at Burgos, two at La Cenia and one in Tauste. However, as late as February 1939, K/88 still retained a few Ju 52/3ms earmarked for night attacks, although there are no details pertaining to such operations.

The last mission to be flown by Ju 52/3m *Behelfsbombers* during the Spanish Civil War took place on 26 March 1939 when *Grupo de Bombardeo Nocturno* 2-G-22, which had been formed to take over German aircraft, was sent to bomb the town of Belmez.

A relatively rare sight – a Ju 52/3m *See* floatplane carrying the emblem of the *Legion Condor*'s *Aufklärungsstaffel See* 88 tethered close to a harbour wall towards the end of the Spanish Civil War. The three-digit fuselage code and the non-standard floats indicate that by the time this photograph was taken, the aircraft may have been passed on to the Spanish

CHAPTER THREE

'WHETHER MEN, FUEL, BOMBS OR BREAD'

Crews of 1./KG 253 undergo instruction in front of a line-up of newly-delivered Ju 52/3ms at Gotha during the late 1930s. Note that some of the men seen here are civilian engineers and technicians, probably from Junkers, available to brief the crews. To the far left of the photograph is a Heinkel He 70

On 1 August 1938 the Luftwaffe's sole specialist transport *Gruppe*, known somewhat misleadingly as a 'Bomber Group for Special Purposes' (KGr.z.b.V.1), which had been formed from IV./KG 152 'Hindenburg' in October 1937 at Fürstenwalde, was split into two new *Gruppen*. The new Ju 52/3m-equipped KGr.z.b.V.1 remained at Fürstenwalde under the command of Oberstleutnant Friedrich-Wilhelm Morzik until October 1938, when it moved to Burg-bei-Magdeburg, while the also newly formed KGr.z.b.V.2, under Oberstleutnant Friedrich-Wilhelm-Kurt von Lindenau, moved to Brandenburg-Briest immediately after its establishment. Each *Gruppe* corresponded to the staff and four companies of a Luftwaffe *Fallschirmjäger* (paratroop) battalion, with four *Staffeln* of 12 Ju 52/3ms each and a *Stab* flight of five aircraft.

By the following year, the Junkers plant at Bernburg and the Allgemeine Transportanlagen GmbH (ATG) at Leipzig were building military versions of the Ju 52/3m (as the 3mg3e and g4e), and in early 1939 the German government instructed Lufthansa to transfer some 50 Ju 52/3m airliners to the Luftwaffe. The aircraft were made available gradually and converted as they arrived into *Behelfsbombers*. After conversion they were assigned to KG.z.b.V.172, a *Geschwader* established by the Berlin-based Air Liaison

Staff and located from August 1939, conveniently, alongside Lufthansa at its main hub at Berlin-Tempelhof.

The *Geschwader* drew its personnel from the airline and was under the command of Oberstleutnant Carl-August Freiherr von Gablenz, an extremely accomplished World War 1 and Lufthansa pilot who, in August 1934, had made an epic, long-distance flight of 14,000 km in a DLH Ju 52/3m from Berlin-Tempelhof, via Belgrade, Athens, Cairo, Baghdad, Calcutta, Bangkok and Canton, to Shanghai. More recently he had made trips to Kabul and Tokyo, but had transferred from the airline to the Luftwaffe in June 1935. Officers of I. and II./KG.z.b.V.172 were subsequently assigned as instructors in blind-flying training at schools at Radom and Wesendorf. In addition a new *Stab* KG.z.b.V.1 (i.e., a *Geschwader* as opposed to a *Gruppe*) was formed at Stendal (see Chapter Four), as was KGr.z.b.V.9 at Eichwalde under Major Torsten-Karl Christ, whose Ju 52/3ms would be used for the transport of heavy weapons. Both these units were formed from personnel drawn from the 'C' twin-engined training schools.

On 1 September 1939 Germany invaded Poland under the codename *Fall Weiss* (Contingency White), an operation that Adolf Hitler had been planning since May of that year on the basis that he believed that Great Britain would not stand by its treaty with Poland. The Luftwaffe was tasked with the destruction of the Polish Air Force and to support German forces on the ground. It was to be a swift and ruthless campaign that saw western Poland taken and the Polish armed forces largely neutralised within the first few days.

A pristine Ju 52/3m in pre-war military markings runs up its engines. The dark paint over the aircraft's nose area, engine cowlings and wheel spats is probably black and the stretched diamonds on the spats, white. The rest of the aircraft would have been in bare metal

Luftwaffe groundcrew and airfield personnel gather around a Ju 52/3m of KG 253 as it takes on fuel from a Standard Oil Company bowser. This view shows to effect the considerable depth of the inner leading edge

Ju 52/3ms played a crucial role in supplying the advancing German armoured units with fuel, food and sufficient ammunition to sustain at least two days' combat capability. The fact was that while the Panzer divisions could carry several days' provisions on their own vehicles, it was fuel that was the Achilles heel. *Luftflotte* 4, under *General der Flieger* Alexander Löhr, which supported Army Group South, assigned one transport *Gruppe*, IV./KG.z.b.V.2, to support General Walther von Reichenau's 10. *Armee*, which was at the spearhead of the German attack. Within two days of operations commencing, the Junkers flew 30 tons of fuel to forward landing strips to supply the tanks of 1. *Panzer Division*, and on the 5th, the quantity increased to 74 tons.

But the need for fuel did not just rest with the Panzers. In the air, support for 10. *Armee* came from Generalmajor von Richthofen, who had returned with some glory from Spain and who was now functioning in his latest assignment as the '*Fliegerführer zur besonderen Verwendung*' (Flying Commander for Special Purposes), a role in which he commanded the bulk of the Ju 87 Stukas acting in direct support of von Reichenau's forces. Von Richthofen's short-range Stukas were jumping from captured airfield to captured airfield, and thus he needed all the transports he could get to keep his dive-bombers supplied with fuel and bombs at their high sortie rates. On 8 September von Richthofen noted;

'Supplies for our units are in danger because a *Transportgruppe* has been set to perform other tasks by the *Luftgau*. There thus exists the danger that we shall have neither fuel nor bombs available at our operational airfields. I protest about this to the *Luftflotte* and hope that they will institute changes to this situation.'

Over the next few days the advance into Poland continued, but for von Richthofen's units, the supply situation had become critical. On the 11th he recorded;

'As previously, there are supply problems. For the Stuka units only one mission can be scheduled. The other units have only enough fuel for a few aircraft. I exert massive pressure on the *Luftgaustab Pflugbeil* [Generalmajor Curt Plugbeil, commander of *Luftgaustab* z.b.V.8], which does everything that has to be done, but which really has insufficient

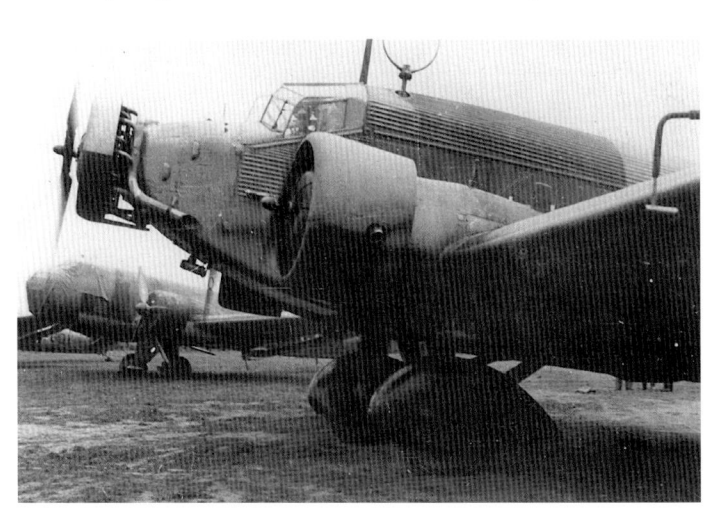

Oberst Alfred Mahncke, the *Kommodore* of KG 152, taxies in a Ju 52/3m at Schwerin while on a visit to II./KG 152 in the autumn of 1938. Two of the *Gruppe*'s Ju 86s can be seen in the background

means. The ground organisation of the Luftwaffe faces very unusual and unexpected tasks, since no-one had reckoned with pursuing a war of continual movement.'

The situation eased somewhat on the 13th when two more *Gruppen* of Ju 52/3ms were allocated to *Luftflotte* 4, and Löhr placed them at the disposal of von Richthofen's forward units, meaning that the Ju 87s could return to flying four or more sorties per day.

One Ju 52/3m unit sent to Poland was *Kampfgruppe z.b.V.9*, which had been formed in mid-August 1939 at Eichwalde, in East Prussia, at Tutow, in Mecklenburg, and other airfields in northern Germany from cadres drawn from various pilot training units and blind-flying schools. It was intended that the *Gruppe* would provide air transport and weapons airlifting for *Fallschirmjäger* units. On 1 September 1939, within a fortnight of its establishment, KGr.z.b.V.9, under the command of Major Christ, moved to Aslau, 90 km west of Breslau, to take part in the attack. Over the course of the next few weeks, the unit's Ju 52/3ms flew transport missions from Aslau, Görlitz and Sagan into Poland in support of ground forces. On just one occasion, on 13 September, KGr.z.b.V.9 carried out an air-landing operation when it ferried paratroopers to Lodz. The swift victory in Poland, however, meant that there was no requirement for large-scale *Fallschirmjäger* operations, and the *Gruppe* was deactivated on 20 October. Its 53 Ju 52/3ms duly returned to the training units from where they had come.

Also on 13 September, under the codename *Unternehmen Wasserkante* (Operation *Water's Edge*), the Luftwaffe had launched a concerted effort to bomb the Polish capital of Warsaw into submission, conducting attacks on key military installations and armament factories in and around the

'Give us our daily bread'. A member of the crew in flying overalls leans against the side door of this Ju 52/3m of III./KG.z.b.V.1 1Z+GW, which has just deposited a load of loaves at an airfield somewhere in Poland. Just visible forward of the cockpit is the unit emblem of 12. *Staffel*, depicting the black bear of the arms of the city of Berlin

Luftwaffe 'black men' – so-called because of their customary black overalls – use a hydraulic bomb trolley to load a heavy crate aboard a Ju 52/3m4ge which still bears what appear to be wide black Lufthansa wing markings, and is thus probably one of the machines handed over to the Luftwaffe by the airline

The lucky ones. Wounded German soldiers aboard a Ju 52/3m 'S' (for *Sanitätsflugzeug*) – a transport that has been adapted for the airborne ambulance role during the Polish campaign of 1939. The men have been tied to the canvas stretchers, which rest on a purpose-built framework, to prevent them from rolling off during flight. Through the cabin door can be seen the central instrument panel in the cockpit

city. Operations had been coordinated mainly by the *Fliegerführer z.b.V.* until Hitler ordered his air commanders to direct their attacks against 'installations essential for the maintenance of life in the city'. It seems that this directive did not entirely satisfy von Richthofen, who, although keen to see his units attack Warsaw 'properly', did not have the necessary assets with which to accomplish his goal.

On 21 September the headquarters of the *Fliegerführer z.b.V.* received orders from *Luftflottenkommando* 4 to the effect that it was to assume overall command for the air strikes against Warsaw – a process that would, in turn, lay a 'clear path' for the army to follow. Von Richthofen wrote;

'We receive orders via the *Flotte* from Ob.d.L. [*Oberbefehlshaber der Luftwaffe* (Commander-in-chief of the Luftwaffe)] that we are tasked to assume leadership of the battle for Warsaw. The Luftwaffe is expected to decisively prepare the way for the Army. For this purpose, we only have light units (Stukas and Do 17s) which cannot even drop incendiary bombs. I request a special He 111 *Geschwader* which will only be used on incendiary missions, otherwise we shall not be able to render the city *Kaputt*. The Ob.d.L. is "amused" about my radio message in which I had asked for the He 111 *Geschwader*.'

But even von Richthofen did not always get what he wanted. On 23 September, as preparations for the bombing of Warsaw were being finalised, he recorded;

Waiting for the go. A line-up of Ju 52/3ms believed to be from KG.z.b.V.2 stand with their loading hatches open in readiness for flight during the Polish campaign. These machines have also been fitted with cockpit gun turrets

'In the afternoon, in accordance with orders, the planned preliminary assault was made ready, but as the clouds are at only 200 m, I had to call it off. The He 111 *Geschwader* that I had requested for dropping incendiaries is turned down. In its stead, Ob.d.L. will place IV./KG.z.b.V.2 [transport Ju 52/3ms] at our disposal for dropping incendiary bombs.'

Von Richthofen may have felt that this was a stopgap or makeshift measure, but in reality, it meant deploying the Ju 52/3m in much the same way as it would have been used in Spain. IV./KG.z.b.V.2 had been formed just a month earlier at Breslau-Gandau under the command of Oberstleutnant Hans Alefeld, who had previously been *Kommandeur* of KGr.z.b.V.5. On 24 September, the *Gruppe*'s Junkers took off from Breslau and landed at Grojek-Kecien, in Poland. However, right to the last, von Richthofen, despite having had plenty of direct experience using Ju 52/3ms as *Behelfsbomber* in Spain, was worried about how the tri-motors would fare over Warsaw. He ordered that a heavy *Flakabteilung* be deployed 'to pin down the flak in Warsaw and to cut our losses'.

The intended 'tactical method' was crude but simple. Von Richthofen recorded;

'For each Ju 52 we assign two groundcrew with potato spades which we obtained from local farms and fields. When a pilot gives the order, the two men are to shovel out the incendiary bombs with the potato spades, as soon as the assault area has been reached. It is, of course, a weird solution, but we can't really do anything else.'

Theory was put into practice on the 25th;

'At 0800 hrs our units go into action to attack Warsaw. We deploy 1150 aircraft and drop 560 tonnes of demolition bombs and 72 tonnes of incendiaries. The effects of incendiaries was immediate everywhere, and soon there was nothing more of the city to be seen. Our "incendiary bombers" flew right across the suburbs of Warsaw and even started a fire in a large, fully-equipped engine factory at Okecie airfield. Everywhere crackled from the incendiary drop. As to be expected, dropping incendiaries from open doors presented problems and resulted in very imprecise drops. One Ju 52, hit by Polish flak, crashed in flames close to Okecie.'

Von Richthofen's fears of greater losses proved to be unfounded. 'We have lost a total of two Ju 52s and one Ju 87!' However, carried by strong northerly winds and as a result of the dispersal of the Junkers' formations, some of the bombs fell behind friendly lines and onto Wehrmacht infantry, inflicting minor casualties. Von Richthofen noted in his diary that the army commanders 'angrily curse at the flyers'. When he later visited the commander of 8. *Armee*, General von Blaskowitz, neither he nor Generaloberst von Brauchitsch, the visiting Commander-in-Chief of the Army, shook his hand. An indignant

The motto on the side of this Ju 52/3m proclaims ominously '1.9.39. Whether people, petrol, bombs or bread, we bring death to Poland'. The aircraft has been fitted with a gun mount for a 7.92 mm MG 15 machine gun above the cockpit to provide additional defence

CHAPTER THREE 'WHETHER MEN, FUEL, BOMBS OR BREAD'

From the doorway of a Ju 52/3m, Generalmajor Hans Jeschonnek, the Chief of the Luftwaffe General Staff, distributes copies of a newspaper to Wehrmacht troops in Poland which probably carries news of the swift German conquest

von Richthofen remarked, 'As was to be expected, I was treated in an extraordinarily unfriendly manner'.

Later that afternoon, von Richthofen flew over Warsaw. The cloud of smoke caused by the incendiaries had reached a height of 3500 m as it drifted off towards the southeast. The war diarist of the *Fliegerführer z.b.V.* noted tersely;

'Incendiary bombing from transport aircraft without sufficient targeting devices cannot be performed successfully. Especially if our own troops are near, no accuracy is guaranteed and our own troops are affected by it.'

On the morning of 27 September the city of Warsaw, many of its buildings destroyed and thousands of its inhabitants having been killed, capitulated. IV./KG.z.b.V.2 relocated back to Breslau and was disbanded in November. As far as is known, the Luftwaffe never again – officially – deployed the Ju 52/3m as a bomber in strength.

Ernst Zindel commented many years later, 'The story put out in post-war accounts in East German newspapers that the Ju 52 had been planned from the outset as a military "terror bomber" is a freely-invented and nonsensical lie. The *Heereswaffenamt*, which for a long time had a secret development and study group for military aircraft, expressed an annihilating verdict on the Ju 52 and determined that as a bomber, it was totally unsuitable'.

Ju 52/3m losses (all causes) for the month of September are listed as 44 aircraft, with a further 15 for the period October-December 1939.

Whilst in general military terms the German attack on Poland can be considered a success, there were shortcomings, not least of which was the highlighted shortage of air transports. It was universally agreed between Luftwaffe leaders that the numbers of available Ju 52/3ms had been insufficient, and that in future operations, these vital aircraft would need to be paramount in any 'war of continual movement'.

A line-up of Ju 52/3ms from an unidentified unit on a misty day at a forward airfield in Poland. The aircraft carry five-digit fuselage codes and early-style national crosses. The white '1' on the aircraft in the foreground is probably a tactical recognition number for use in formation flights

CHAPTER FOUR

ATTACK IN THE NORTH

The reasons for the adverse shortage of German transport aircraft in Poland can perhaps be attributed to the philosophy that prevailed within the senior operations command of the Luftwaffe during the late 1930s. At that time, Luftwaffe planners envisaged the prime need for transports being centred around the movement and dropping, or landing, of paratroops, while the supply of aircraft to *Luftflotten* for supply work was more limited when set against the concept of fast, short campaigns – or so-called '*Blitzkriege*'– where objectives would be taken quickly by superior forces. As a result of this philosophy, only a relatively small number of Ju 52/3ms was allocated for general transport, and even for the paratroop and air-landing operations it was felt that aircraft could be brought in from training units on an 'as needed' basis. German planners had taken note of Italian operations in Ethiopia, where unit mobility had been crucial, and during the course of 1939 most first-line Luftwaffe units were assigned two Ju 52/3ms for transport and/or deployment as radio or direction-finding aircraft.

Earlier, however, on 7 November 1938, the *Generalstab der Luftwaffe* issued a target for the Luftwaffe to include four *Transportgeschwader* numbering 500 aircraft, but by the end of August of that year, a revised figure of 552 Ju 52/3m transports was set as an acceptable number with which the Luftwaffe could function. Then, in its *Flugzeugbeschaffungs-Programm* Nr. 11 of 1 April 1939, the RLM projected a requirement of

German troops prepare to lift boxes of machine gun ammunition, having been landed at an airfield in either Norway or Denmark by Ju 52/3m transports

2260 Ju 52/3ms running to 1 April 1942, but just three months later, on 5 August, Göring decreed that production was to be cut back in favour of the development of new combat aircraft such as the He 177, Ju 88, Me 210 and Bf 109. Thus a revised total of 1400 Ju 52/3ms was to be built up to April 1942, with production capped at just 15 per month thereafter.

By 1940, the fact that the Ju 52/3m had remained in production in significant numbers throughout the late 1930s as a *Behelfsbomber* while the RLM awaited delivery of its new generation of bombers meant that the Luftwaffe had more than 1000 such aircraft with which to form a specialist transport force. Aircraft supply and lift capability was not, therefore, viewed as a problem when the Luftwaffe undertook its first major *Fallschirmjäger* and air-landing operations.

There was little need for internal adaptation of the Ju 52/3m to become a transport for the *Fallschirmjäger*. Furthermore, not only were crews and ground personnel in the Ju 52/3m units trained in the art of handling, loading, stowing and unloading army equipment without the risk of damage, but also in packing and even rigging parachutes. Under the conversion designation '*Ausführung F*', early aircraft even retained the ventral gun turret and some of their bomb racks, but later, with the turret removed, it was standard for between 12 and 18 paratroops to be seated in the fuselage facing inwards on canvas seats fitted to the fuselage walls. Thus, a *Staffel* with a nominal strength of 12 aircraft could deliver 156 men, and the four *Staffeln* of a transport *Gruppe*, a battalion. The exit door was in the rear port side of the aircraft and a horn or buzzer would sound just ahead of the drop zone to prepare the *Fallschirmjäger* to jump. A red light would flash indicating the actual time to jump.

As a Ju 52/3m approached the designated drop zone (DZ), an *Absetzer* (dispatcher) ordered the men to their feet. The *Absetzer* represented a replacement for the observer in a standard military crew, which also included pilot, flight engineer, radio operator and gunner. The paratroops then turned into a line facing the back of the aircraft looking towards the exit door, with each man clenching the snap-hook end of his static line in his teeth so as to leave his hands free. On instruction from the *Absetzer* the static line from the parachute was hooked to a strong wire metal cable running high along the fuselage wall, and along which the hook would run as the 'stick' of men made their way to the door. As a paratrooper reached the door, he braced himself, feet apart and hands grasping the door frame, before launching himself outwards and away from the Ju 52/3m. The parachute was automatically pulled from its bag and opened by the static line at nine metres from the aircraft when fully extended. The static line and bag would then break away under the man's falling weight and momentum, and would remain dangling from the Junkers' door.

Because their harnesses were carried on their backs, the *Fallschirmjäger* would adopt a spread-eagled jump and dive position as they threw themselves from the Ju 52/3m in order to reduce both swing in the air and the shock-jolt from the static line. A quick opening of the canopy countered swing and

Trainee navigators undergo instruction in a Ju 52 *Hörsaalflugzeug* ('classroom aircraft'). The pupils sit at fold-down tables plotting courses, with instructions being received in their earphones. The instructor sits at the console at the rear of the fuselage. Note the framework of the dorsal machine gun turret beneath the corrugated roof which has been closed off

enabled a more controlled descent. During initial parachute operations, the parachutist would jump armed only with a pistol and hand grenade, some ammunition and essential rations for three days, and it was intended that he would recover his other weapons from containers that were dropped at the same time. The containers, which from 1941 were dropped using different coloured parachutes, were usually stowed on specially installed racks inside the cargo holds of the Ju 52/3ms.

The *Fallschirmjäger* would not take to their parachutes in action until the spring of 1940. As early as October 1939, Admiral Erich Raeder had warned Hitler of the consequences of a British occupation of Norway. But if Norway could be occupied and secured before that eventuality, then German access to Swedish iron ore and other important raw materials would be secured. Norway could also offer valuable bases for German U-boats and for air-sea operations against the Arctic convoys. Conversely, any British presence in Norway would provide the RAF with airfields from which to bomb northern Germany, as well as offering the Royal Navy an opportunity to get into the Baltic.

In December 1939 Hitler had issued the first instructions for a German operation against Norway to be studied, but on 16 February 1940 his hand was forced when a Royal Naval destroyer intercepted the German prison ship *Altmark* in Norwegian territorial waters. This was the clearest evidence yet that the Norwegians were powerless to prevent either Britain or Germany intervening at will in Norwegian waters. On 2 April, Hitler, wanting to pre-empt any British initiative, gave his commanders the order that an invasion of Norway and also Denmark – where the seizure of key airfields would be imperative to the success of operations farther north – was to begin in five days' time under the code name *Weserübung*. The German plan was for a quick strike in a combined operation deploying air and naval forces against Norway's most important coastal cities, from Oslo in the south to Narvik in the north, as well as the two main airports at Oslo and Stavanger, which were to be captured by airborne troops. In addition, key coastal points and airfields at Aalborg, in North Jutland, and Vordingborg, 80 km to the southwest of Copenhagen, in Denmark, would be captured.

Placed under the control of Generalleutnant Hans Geisler's X. *Fliegerkorps* was the *Lufttransportchef Land*, a specialist transport command led by Oberstleutnant von Gablenz which comprised eight *Gruppen*. The *Stab* KG.z.b.V.1 (*Kampfgeschwader zur besonderen Verwendung* – Bomb Wing for Special Purposes) was formed at Stendal on 26 August 1939 under Oberstleutnant Fritz Morzik, but the unit's title was misleading for what was viewed officially as being a *Transportfliegergeschwader* equipped primarily with Ju 52/3ms.

Each of the *Geschwader*'s *Gruppen* had a nominal strength of 53 Ju 52/3ms, totalling 212 aircraft in all. The *Stab* counted one Junkers and a liaison aircraft. The I. *Gruppe* was raised at Gardelegen from KGr.z.b.V.1, which in turn had been formed at Fürstenwalde from IV./KG 152 and placed

Technicians operate a bank of dials and gauges that have been built into a Ju 52/3m either for works-testing or for scientific purposes. Just visible at far left through the doorway to the cockpit is the pilot adjusting the heating of the aircraft

under the command of Major Dr. Max Ziervogel. II./KG.z.b.V.1 was also established at Stendal under Hauptmann Friedrich-Wilhelm-Kurt von Lindenau from elements of KGr.z.b.V.2, while III. *Gruppe* shared the same place of formation and origins and was led by Hauptmann Markus Zeidler. A IV. *Gruppe* was newly formed at the same time under Major Johannes Janzen.

Stab/KG.z.b.V.2 had been established at Küpper-Sagan under Oberstleutnant Karl Drewes on the same day as *Stab*/KG.z.b.V.1 and was commanded by former World War 1 infantry officer Oberst Dipl.-Ing. Gerhard Conrad, who had previously led I./KG 257. It too was equipped with Ju 52/3ms. The *Geschwader*'s component *Gruppen* were all newly formed on 26 August 1939 at Sorau (I. *Gruppe* – Hauptmann Hans-Eberhard Freiherr von Hornstein), Freiwaldau (II. and III. *Gruppen* – Oberstleutnant Rudolf Stoltenhoff and Major Neudörffer, respectively) and Breslau-Gandau (IV. *Gruppe* – Oberstleutnant Hans Alefeld).

These *Geschwader* were augmented under the *Lufttransportchef Land* by eight *Kampfgruppen zur besonderen Verwendung* (Bomb Groups for Special Purposes), all of which had been newly formed in March 1940 with a *Stab* and four *Staffeln*, and which comprised KG.z.b.V.101 (Oberstleutnant Ernst Mundt) at Neumünster, KGr.z.b.V.102 (Oberst Wilhelm Baur de Betaz) at Oldenburg, KGr.z.b.V.103 (Hauptmann Richard Wagner) at Schleswig, KGr.z.b.V.104 (Major von Jena) at Stade, KGr.z.b.V.105 (Major Dannenberg) at Kiel-Holtenau, KGr.z.b.V.106 (Oberstleutnant Hugo Stolt) at Ütersen, KGr.z.b.V.107 at Fuhlsbüttel and KGr.z.b.V.108 (possibly under Hauptmann Förster) at Rantum and Hörnum, on Sylt. With the exception of KGr.z.b.V.105, which included a small number of Ju 52/3ms as well as Ju 90 and Fw 200 four-engined transports, and KGr.z.b.V.108, which was equipped with Ju 52/3m *See* and other seaplanes, this force was made up entirely of standard Ju 52/3m transports. Each *Gruppe* numbered 53 Ju 52/3ms.

It would be the bulk of Morzik's KG.z.b.V.1, having moved to Ütersen, Schleswig, Stade and Hagenow, that would carry the *Fallschirmjäger* to Scandinavia on the morning of 9 April. That morning the German government had served the Norwegian and Danish governments with its intention of embarking on military action, and as the Luftwaffe's transports commenced their flights they were informed that while Denmark would accept occupation, Norway would not.

A column of Wehrmacht infantrymen march past several parked Ju 52/3ms on a grass airfield at the commencement of operations against Norway. To the left of the foreground is a Klemm Kl 35 trainer

Operations against Denmark, therefore, went off smoothly and without opposition under cloudless skies, although just 36 hours before the operation was to start, a decision was taken to extract 90 paratroops from the Aalborg force and to deploy them from nine Ju 52/3ms south of Copenhagen from where they would seize the three-kilometre-long Stoerstrom bridge linking a ferry terminal on Falster to Seeland and, eventually, the capital, until the arrival of infantry. Within minutes of landing the Germans had captured the local garrison on the little island of Masnedö, and by 0700 hrs the bridge had been taken as well.

Escorted by Bf 110s, Ju 52/3ms of 8./KG.z.b.V.1 dropped parachutists close to Aalborg-West in order to cover the landing of further aircraft from I., II. and III./KG.z.b.V.1 as they air-landed troops. The drop went faultlessly and Luftwaffe fighters were soon flying into the field, using it as a forward base less than two hours later.

However, not everything went so smoothly. Major Karl Drewes, an experienced World War 1 aviator leading 29 Ju 52/3ms from 3. and 6./KG.z.b.V.1, became concerned at the steadily thickening fog over the Skagerrak as his formation made its way to Oslo-Fornebu. As he neared the Oslo Fjord, two of his aircraft disappeared into the fog and he decided to turn back and to make for Aalborg, despite the fact that his well-meant decision would have risky consequences for the second wave of Oslo-bound Ju 52/3m transports assigned to land more *Fallschirmjäger* on the ground there on the assumption that the airport had already been seized by paratroops.

Heading for Stavanger-Sola were 12 Ju 52/3ms of 7./KG.z.b.V.1 under Hauptmann Günther Capito, carrying more *Fallschirmjäger*. Capito also encountered severely adverse weather over the sea off the west coast of Norway. He pressed on, however, and after some 30 minutes the weather cleared, but his Junkers were scattered and one was missing. It took another 30 minutes for the remainder to form up again and head north, low above the waves, en route for the drop.

At 0920 hrs the Junkers turned to cross the coast and head inland along a valley at just a few metres above the ground in order to maintain surprise. Climbing to 120 m and clearing some hills, the Ju 52/3ms were then over the DZ. The pilots throttled back to reduce speed and, maintaining their height of 120 m, the doors were opened. Within a matter of seconds the *Fallschirmjäger* had jumped and their weapons containers dropped soon after them. The Ju 52/3ms then turned, went back down to just ten metres and at full throttle made their exit. The drop was successful, and with the support of Luftwaffe fighters and bombers, Sola airfield was quickly captured.

Once the initial paratroop objectives had been successfully taken the immediate priority was to get more troops on the ground to consolidate the German assault. But again there were problems. At Oslo-Fornebu, although the *Fallschirmjäger* had not dropped because of fog, a second wave of Ju 52/3ms from KGr.z.b.V.103 carrying more paratroops to be air-landed was subsequently on its way to land at what was an unsecured airport. Despite Generalleutnant Geisler ordering a recall, Oberstleutnant von Gablenz was confident in the ability of his transport crews to deal with the situation and argued, 'They can force a landing even though the airfield has not been secured'.

Believed to be Ju 52/3m TJ+AU, this aeroplane is seen at Oslo in April 1940. The aircraft has had large wing crosses applied for ease of recognition in the air, and the *Hakenkreuz* has been applied over both tail and rudder

Gablenz's stubborn optimism eventually paid off, but only after the *Kommandeur* of the KGr.z.b.V.103 formation, over which he had direct responsibility, Hauptmann Richard Wagner, was killed and a number of his men wounded when his aircraft was raked by gunfire from the ground as it came in to land. Wagner, whose pilots numbered several experienced instructors well able to cope with the fog, had believed that the signal to turn back from Geisler was an enemy ruse. However, with Wagner dead, the pilot of his Ju 52/3m promptly opened up his throttle and climbed away as fast as he could. Nevertheless, with fog still lingering, one by one, the other Junkers came down, some without difficulty, while others, having been hit by ground fire, crash-landed amidst wrecked German and Norwegian aircraft that already littered the airfield. After quelling the local resistance, however, the main force of 159 Ju 52/3ms began ferrying in troops and Luftwaffe ground staff, as well as supplies and equipment.

Ironically, at the time of the German landings at Fornebu, Ju 52/3m, Wk-Nr 5881 G-AFAP *Jason*, operated by British Airways, happened to be at the airport and about to depart for England. The British aircraft was not permitted to leave and was subsequently confiscated by the Germans, while its crew managed to escape to Sweden.

To the far north around Narvik, the mountain troops of Generalleutnant Eduard Dietl's 3. *Gebirgs-Division* had been isolated following their landing there on 9 April. The harbour at Narvik had been blocked by the Royal Navy and the city was in British hands, with much German equipment, ammunition and food supplies being lost in the process. At first, formations of Ju 52/3ms from KGr.z.b.V.107 and KGr.z.b.V.108, fitted with auxiliary fuel tanks to provide sufficient range, carried out supply flights from airfields to the south to the hills around Narvik. Inherently, however, the additional tanks introduced weight and took away cargo-carrying space, but they did drop supplies loaded into *Fallschirmjäger* containers or simply pushed crates directly out of the fuselage. The problem was that no heavy weapons – badly needed by Dietl's troops – could be transported and dropped this way, although a radical solution was devised. It was to be a calculated gamble and also a tribute to aircrews who undertook the risk.

On 13 April, the day following the destruction of the German destroyers that had ferried the *Gebirgs-Division* to Narvik, 16 Ju 52/3ms of Oberst Wilhelm Baur de Betaz's KGr.z.b.V.102 at Oslo-Fornebu were loaded up to full capacity with the 75 mm Skoda artillery guns and personnel of the 112. *Gebirgs-Artillerie-Regiment*, together with as much ammunition as they could carry – but less the auxiliary tanks used previously. Dietl had identified a frozen lake, Lake Hartvig, near Bardufoss and some 110 km north-northeast of Narvik, as a potential landing ground for the Ju 52/3ms. After weighing up the risks and the benefits, it was decided that the Junkers would carry only enough fuel to reach the lake. Three further

Ju 52/3ms would follow on, laden with fuel to be used for the return flight to Oslo. In addition to the transports, one Junkers was fitted out as a communications aircraft to signal the progress of the operation. At 0845 hrs the Ju 52/3ms took off and headed northwards.

As the heavily laden formation reached Narvik and flew in low over the Ofot Fjord, so they attracted fire from the fleet of British warships assembled off the coast. Five Ju 52/3ms were hit and two of them crashed. The remaining force managed to reach Hartvig and land on the lake, but because of the spring thaw, eight aircraft cracked the ice and sustained damage. The communications aircraft signalled that only two machines could be considered in good enough order to make the return flight, but since the transports carrying the fuel had not arrived, this would not be possible. Nevertheless, for Dietl, the arrival of the Ju 52/3ms was 'a welcome sight'.

Despite a general lack of supplies, intense cold and deep snow, Dietl's small force managed to hold out and even retake Narvik in June when Britain abandoned its efforts to evict the Germans from Norway owing to German successes on the Western Front. For their part, the Ju 52/3ms on Lake Hartvig were abandoned and sank in the spring thaw. Generalmajor a.D. Fritz Morzik opined, 'The incidental fact that the desired end was attained should not be accepted as evidence for the establishment of a general principle. The air transport of a mountain battery, in the prior realisation that all of the participating Ju 52s would be lost, can be viewed only as a last, desperate measure'.

On 14 April a formation of 15 Ju 52/3ms from II./KG.z.b.V.1 carried a force of 160 *Fallschirmjäger* to the town of Dombås in the Gudbrandsdal Valley, 350 km northwest of Oslo and 200 km south of Trondheim, which was judged by Hitler to be a key point on the Oslo–Trondheim railway and a base from which to prevent the joining of Allied forces that had landed at Andalsnes and Norwegian forces withdrawing from Oslo, in central Norway. The reality, however, was that the operation had been put together hurriedly and with little planning, with the intention to supply 160 paratroops from the air once they had taken Dombås, and where they were to wait until German ground forces arrived to relieve them.

On 13 April 1940 16 Ju 52/3ms of KGr.z.b.V.102 used the frozen Lake Hartvig, near Bardufoss in northern Norway, as a landing ground. The Junkers were carrying troops and guns of a mountain artillery regiment. After landing, some of the aircraft managed to stay afloat as the ice cracked and melted through the use of empty fuel drums, as seen in the case of Wk-Nr 6821 VB+UP of 1. or 3./KGr.z.b.V.102 in the foreground in this photograph. Note the Junkers in the background that has not been so fortunate

Four groundcrew gather for a snapshot in front of a Ju 52/3m that has been parked on typical wooden planking as used on mud, ice and snow-covered airfields in the far north for adhesion

Once again, the Junkers ran into bad weather over the target area which steadily worsened as their pilots desperately searched for the DZ. The ground defences were alerted and one Junkers was hit, which force-landed, killing several paratroops on board, while another seven aircraft gave up and returned home. But even of these, four were subsequently badly damaged and another came down in Sweden. Some of the *Fallschirmjäger* were dropped over Dombås, but at too low a height and several were killed, including the force commander. Just 45 men survived the flight and the jump to fight on the ground with the aim of blocking the road and inflicting damage to the transport infrastructure, which they did. But, becoming increasingly cold and isolated, they surrendered six days later.

Nevertheless, in retrospect, the Dombås operation does not overshadow the swift, efficiently executed and successful parachute drops elsewhere in Scandinavia on 9 April.

Meanwhile, on 20 April, Ju 52/3ms were also active farther south along the Norwegian coast at Trondheim, where 90 aircraft air-landed hundreds of infantry and mountain troops. On the 23rd and 24th, 120 Junkers ferried in even more reinforcements, including Flak troops and equipment.

Ju 52/3ms would remain operating in Norway in the weeks immediately after the German assault. Following a request from *Luftflotte* 5, a *Transportgruppe z.b.V.* was formed in June 1940 that took on around ten Ju 52/3ms previously on the strength of KGr.z.b.V.106.

Ultimately, by the conclusion of operations in Norway, the 617 Luftwaffe transports that took part in the campaign had flown 3018 sorties in which they dropped or landed 2376 tons of supplies and 29,280 personnel for the loss of a third of their number. Despite that loss rate, in Operation *Weserübung* the Luftwaffe had proved that its Ju 52/3ms and its *Fallschirmjäger* would be a force to reckoned with.

Meanwhile, during April, changes had been in progress, which saw KGr.z.b.V.103 deactivated and the bulk of the aircraft of KGr.z.b.V.102 reassigned to training schools with the aim of increasing the number of trained crews available to operational units.

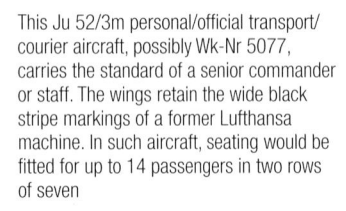

This Ju 52/3m personal/official transport/courier aircraft, possibly Wk-Nr 5077, carries the standard of a senior commander or staff. The wings retain the wide black stripe markings of a former Lufthansa machine. In such aircraft, seating would be fitted for up to 14 passengers in two rows of seven

CHAPTER FIVE

ATTACK IN THE WEST

The success of the paratroop landings in Norway and Denmark had proven their effectiveness as a means of assault. Within a matter of weeks, paratroop and air-landing operations would be used once again to achieve German military objectives in the West. In February 1940, weeks before *Weserübung* had commenced, the German High Command had finalised its plan for the invasion of France and the Low Countries, to be known as *Fall Gelb* (Contingency Yellow). The aim was for Generaloberst Wilhelm von Leeb's *Heeresgruppe* C (Army Group C) to hold the Franco-German border opposite the Maginot Line, while Generaloberst Gerd von Rundstedt's *Heeresgruppe* A made the main attack, with the bulk of the German armour, through the forests of the Ardennes, in southern Belgium, and Luxembourg. Simultaneously, Generaloberst Fedor von Bock's *Heeresgruppe* B was to mount a secondary advance through northern Belgium and southern Holland to draw the main British and French forces north so that von Rundstedt could hit their flank.

Heeresgruppe B included in its order of battle 18. *Armee* which, in turn, mustered the airborne forces of Generalleutnant Kurt Student's 7. *Fliegerdivision* and the Wehrmacht's 22. *Luftlande-Infanterie Division*. These formations were to be dropped by parachute and air-landed in the Netherlands in order to tie down enemy forces. They were also to capture and hold key bridges and to destroy Dutch strongholds. Once relieved by advancing German ground forces, these units would be

A Ju 52/3m delivers a string of German *Fallschirmjäger* over The Netherlands in May 1940

In a photograph probably dating from 1938 or 1939, NCO instructors watch as trainee paratroops pull on and buckle their harnesses while their packed parachutes lie on the ground around them. Behind them are the Ju 52/3ms, carrying pre-war five-digit fuselage codes, which will take them up for their jump

A parachutist jumps from a Ju 52/3m, flying only a few hundred metres above the ground, his static line still attached, while being filmed by an observer standing in the gun turret and watched by civilians from the road below. A second *Fallschirmjäger* prepares to jump from the fuselage door

subordinated to 18. *Armee* for the duration of the ground fighting. The planning and preparation for these operations were detailed and given considerable thought. Returning from Scandinavia, the Ju 52/3m *Gruppen* had their losses replaced and were bolstered by fresh crews, and on 8 May 1940 they moved to airfields in northwest Germany, where they were joined by the paratroops of *Fallschirmjäger-Regiment* I. The Ju 52/3m units assigned to 7. *Fliegerdivision* on 10 May comprised Oberstleutnant Morzik's KG.z.b.V.1 with four *Gruppen* at Loddenheide, Werl and Handorf, numbering 213 aircraft, of which 208 were serviceable, and *Stab*/KG.z.b.V.2 under Oberstleutnant Karl Drewes which was a composite command made up of KGr.z.b.V.9 at Lippspringe, KGr.z.b.V.11 at Lippstadt, KGr.z.b.V.12 at Störmede and 1./KGr.z.b.V.172 at Paderborn. This formation fielded 211 Ju 52/3ms, of which 204 were serviceable. Additionally, 17./KGr.z.b.V.5 at Köln, which was an element of the special assault unit *Sturmabteilung Koch*, had 52 Junkers, of which 48 were serviceable, as well as DFS 230 assault gliders and He 111 tugs. Thus, aircraft availability levels were high.

The initial German deployment came when airborne troops carried out an audacious glider-borne assault on the Belgian fortress at Eben-Emael, on the Albert Canal, on 10 May. Eben-Emael was the northernmost and most powerful fortification of the Maginot Line, guarding Liège and the Albert Canal against an attack from the east (in other words, from Germany). It had been built into a steep cliff just five years earlier after the canal had been dynamited. Triangular in shape, it measured 820 m on its canal and inland elevations, by 640 m on its northward elevation, and was protected by a vast, sheer and unconquerable cutting 36 m deep that fell straight into the canal. The fort's various single and double turrets bristled with 18 artillery pieces ranging in size from 75 mm to 120 mm guns in casemates two metres thick. There were also numerous light cannon, anti-tank and machine guns.

Its guns would pin down any enemy assault mounted towards the canal and the three bridges crossing it just west of Maastricht. It housed, deep within its concrete walls, a battalion of troops who occupied 48 km of corridors and stairways.

The fort even boasted an internal railway system. Its two 'weak' points, however, were its lack of AA defence and its unmined surfaces.

Away to the east, in Germany, throughout early 1940, this information had become very well known to the senior members of the highly trained *Fallschirmjäger* unit known as the *Sturmabteilung Koch*. St.Abt. *Koch* had been established by Student with the specific tasks of capturing Eben-Emael and the three bridges over the canal in a swift and audacious airborne landing operation as the opening spearhead move for *Fall Gelb*. Named after its commander, Hauptmann Walter Koch, a tough paratroop officer and former security policeman, the unit numbered just under 450 men based at Hildesheim, where they undertook their training. With all leave cancelled, Koch's unit had spent weeks at Hildesheim shrouded in secrecy and cut off from contact with the outside world while they studied every aspect of their objectives and mission.

The *Abteilung* was composed of four *Sturmgruppen* (assault groups) – '*Eisen*' (Iron) under Oberleutnant Schächter, '*Stahl*' (Steel) under Oberleutnant Altmann, '*Beton*' (Concrete) under Leutnant Schacht and '*Granit*' (Granite) under Oberleutnant Witzig. *Eisen* was to take the bridge at Canne, *Stahl* the Veldvezelt bridge, *Beton* was to target the Vroenhoven bridge while *Granit*, with 85 men, had as its objective Eben-Emael.

Following the successful capture of the bridges and the fortress, the *Sturmabteilung* was to hold its objectives until relieved by the advancing Panzers of General von Reichenau's 6. *Armee*. But unlike the *Fallschirmjäger* taking the bridges in Holland, those heading for the Albert Canal would make their assault in a force of 42 DFS 230 gliders belonging to 17./KGr.z.b.V.5. For this mission, the *Staffel*, which had been formed at Hildesheim in October 1939 from the *Lastensegler-Versuchszug* and incorporated into St.Abt. *Koch*, was reorganised into four semi-autonomous glider *Staffeln* – 1.(*Granit*) under Leutnant Hans Schweitzer, 2.(*Eisen*) under Leutnant Seide, 3.(*Beton*) under Oberleutnant Hans-Günther Nevries and 4.(*Stahl*), led by Oberleutnant Walter-Heinz Steinweg.

A force of 42 Ju 52/3ms of Hauptmann Markus Zeidler's III./KG.z.b.V.1 would tow the gliders from Köln-Ostheim towards their respective targets. *Sturmgruppen Stahl* and *Eisen* had each been assigned ten DFS 230s while *Beton* and *Granit* each numbered 11 gliders.

In the afternoon of 9 May, on receipt of orders from VIII. *Fliegerkorps*, St.Abt. *Koch* departed Hildesheim for the Köln area. Around 1800 hrs the Ju 52/3ms of III./KG.z.b.V.1 arrived at Köln-Ostheim and Köln-Butzweilerhof, where the DFS 230s had been since January, having been moved there in furniture lorries and assembled by a special advance detachment. By 0100 hrs on 10 May all the Ju 52/3ms and DFS 230s had been

Fallschirmjäger quickly pull a trolley away from a Ju 52/3m aircraft. The men all wear jump smocks and standard paratroop helmets. Note the chipped paintwork on the tail *Hakenkreuz*

Fallschirmjäger jump at low level from the fuselage door of a Ju 52/3m in what might be a training flight or an exercise. Note the absence of a dorsal gunner and the equipment canister attached to the lowest parachute

coupled and the gliders were loaded with equipment, after which the *Fallschirmjäger* climbed aboard. Then, from 0430 hrs, the Ju 52/3m–DFS 230 *Schleppzüge* (tow units) took off from Ostheim (1., 2., and 3. *Staffeln* of DFS 230s) and Butzweilerhof (4. *Staffel*) and set off on a southerly course, past Köln, gaining height as they climbed at 150 km/h.

Once the correct altitude had been attained the aircraft adopted their operational formation, with each *Staffel* divided into two groups of between four and six *Schleppzüge*, and commenced their approach run to the objectives. Because, in the interest of surprise, strict radio silence was to be observed, the crews of the Ju 52/3ms received no navigational directions but instead followed a chain of flaming beacons in the darkness that directed them towards the Dutch/German border.

The two airfield formations linked at a point west of Köln between Frechen and Bottenboich. They then flew a direct 57-km course towards the border at 170 km/h, passing over a string of searchlights and rotating beacons. En route, however, there were two potentially catastrophic mishaps. Firstly, in the darkness just south of Köln, the pilot of one Ju 52/3m suddenly spotted the exhaust flames of another Junkers directly in front of him. Unless immediate evasive action was taken, his aircraft would collide with the other. The pilot pushed his aircraft into a dive, but the pilot of the glider he was towing struggled to equalise the tension on the tow cable. Seconds later the cable snapped with a crack against the DFS 230's canopy, and with the engines of the Ju 52/3ms fading, the glider pilot had no alternative but to turn back and land at Köln. Amongst those in this particular DFS 230 was Oberleutnant Rudolf Witzig, the commander of the pioneer company from II. *Fallschirmjäger-Regiment* (FJR) 1 and leader of *Sturmgruppe Granit*, and his men, who were tasked with landing on Eben-Emael and capturing it.

Twenty minutes later, the pilot of another Ju 52/3m waggled his aircraft's wings and blinked his position lights (the signal to detach) in error as his *Schleppzug* passed Lucherburg – the site of another beacon just over halfway to the border. Although uncertain and confused, the pilot of the glider conformed to the signal and uncoupled to come down in a field near Düren. The *Fallschirmjäger* resorted to requisitioning cars and driving to the border.

Meanwhile, an anxious Oberleutnant Witzig and his team had landed in a meadow just east of the Rhine. As they clambered out of their glider, with considerable initiative, Witzig ordered his men to convert the meadow into a makeshift airfield while he would try to locate a spare Ju 52/3m. Fortunately, catching a car to Ostheim, he then discovered that no more Junkers were available there. He was then forced to call the airfield at Gütersloh to check there. It was 0505 hrs and *Granit* was down to nine gliders.

It took the rest of the formation 31 minutes to reach the Vetschauer Berg north of Aachen, where the *Schleppzüge* were due to uncouple at 2600 m. From there the glider *Staffeln* would split up and glide towards their respective targets between 24.5 and 29.5 km away. The reality was that the formation had reached this point about ten minutes ahead of schedule because of stronger than anticipated tail winds, which also meant that the *Schleppzüge* were 450 m lower than the assigned uncoupling height. The detaching actually took place over Holland between the border and Maastricht, at which point the DFS 230s dipped slightly, but their pilots made corrections to take them with a trim of a 1-in-12 glide towards their targets.

After some difficulties, the operation went on to become a success. First down at 0515 hrs was the *Beton* group at Vroenhoven, which came under heavy fire during its approach. Schacht's section was engaged in some fierce fighting with the Belgians for the rest of the day, but held out until they were relieved by an army infantry battalion. The *Gruppe* lost ten men in its assault, with a further 29 wounded.

Sturmgruppe Stahl and the remaining gliders of *Granit* landed almost simultaneously at around 0520 hrs. At the Veldvezelt bridge, the Belgians had inexplicably removed their demolition charges and the *Fallschirmjäger* had seized it within 15 minutes. However, the Germans then had to fight off several counter-attacks during the day until they were relieved at 2130 hrs. *Stahl* would suffer eight men dead and 30 wounded. *Granit* was over Eben-Emael at 0520 hrs, the sudden, silent appearance of the DFS 230s on the roof of the fortress causing total surprise to its occupants. Indeed, the gliders were fired on only as they neared the ground. In the absence of Witzig, the *Fallschirmjäger*, led by an NCO and under covering machine gun fire from the gliders, attacked the fortress with flame-throwers and hollow-charge demolition devices. Within minutes, seven casemates and 14 guns had been disabled and the paratroops had entered the fortress.

Oberleutnant Witzig finally landed at 0830 hrs, having secured the services of another Ju 52/3m, and took charge of the operation. Again, there were Belgian counter-attacks, and the paratroops had to take cover in the captured casemates until they too were relieved by an engineer battalion on the morning of the 11th, after which they went on to take all of Eben-Emael. Only six of Witzig's team of 85 were killed in the operation, although 20 were wounded.

Eisen did not fare so well. A Wehrmacht motorised column had already reached the Canne bridge ahead of schedule, with the result that it caused the Belgians to demolish it. The *Fallschirmjäger* here also subsequently came in to land under heavy fire. Their leader, Schächter, was killed in the fighting, but his men fought off two counter-attacks until they were relieved late in the evening.

However, with the detaching of the gliders over Holland, the day's activities were still not quite over for III./KG.z.b.V.1. Arriving at a pre-determined drop point, the Ju 52/3ms released their tow cables and turned once again towards the west. Passing over Eben-Emael, they headed into Belgium. Forty kilometres west of the Albert Canal, the Ju 52/3ms opened their fuselage doors and their crews pushed out a total of 200 uniformed straw dummies attached to parachutes and self-igniting charges that were meant to create the sound of gunfire. When they reached the latest German DZ, the local Belgian forces, alarmed and confused, realised that they had fallen victim to an elaborate enemy decoy operation.

Following these opening moves, once their gliders had been released, the other Ju 52/3m tugs turned back to their bases, with most going to

Gymnich, 15 km southwest of Köln, where, in another elaborate deception operation, they were reloaded with 400 more dummy paratroopers. With the latter on board, 50 Ju 52/3ms flew back over Maastricht, together with a fighter escort, and released their loads between St Trond and Tirlemont. The moment of release had been selected on the assumption that, by then, the Belgian reserves would have received the alarm and would be under way to the scene of the 'drop'. This deception proved a success. A Belgian motorised formation, which had been assigned to launch a counter-attack against the *Fallschirmjäger* on the Albert Canal bridgeheads, changed its plans midway to its original destination in order to meet the new 'enemy landing'. By the time the Belgians realised they had been the victims of a deceptive manoeuvre, the decisive moment had passed and they arrived too late at the Albert Canal.

Following on immediately from the Eben-Emael operation, the *Fallschirmjäger* of 7. *Fliegerdivision* were flown in by Ju 52/3ms over the area of the Netherlands known as 'Fortress Holland'. Here, the relatively small Dutch Army had concentrated its forces. The area was protected to the south by the Rhine-Maas estuary and to the east by the Zuider Zee, and contained the major cities of Rotterdam, Amsterdam, The Hague and Utrecht. Hitler and his senior planning staff knew that Holland had to be conquered as quickly as possible to prevent any meaningful Allied counter-response and to release German units quickly for deployment in Belgium. To do this, key bridges over the southern Rhine-Maas estuary would need to be taken intact, including the 1200-m-long road viaduct and a 1280-m railway bridge over the Holland Deep (the Diep) at Moerdijk, another over the Oude Maas at Dordrecht, as well as bridges leading into Rotterdam over the Nieuwe Maas. Their capture would allow speedy movement of German Panzer units towards Rotterdam. Once the latter was taken it was foreseen that 'Fortress Holland' would capitulate.

The *Fallschirmjäger* were tasked to hold the bridges for up to five days until the arrival of more airborne units, which would land in Ju 52/3ms at Waalhaven airport, eight kilometres south of Rotterdam. This meant that that the airport would also have to be taken if the air-landings were to proceed without trouble.

Following soon after a heavy aerial bombardment by He 111s on Waalhaven, which destroyed many of the airport's hangars as well as Dutch positions around the field, Zeidler's transports carrying the men of III./FJR 1 went in, guided by the billowing smoke from the bombed airport buildings. All the Ju 52/3ms assigned to the airborne operations that day had taken off in *Ketten* (three-aircraft groups) at carefully pre-planned times, then assembled in a circling climb and set course for their DZs in a javelin formation by *Gruppen* in order to cross the Dutch border in a broad formation. Generalmajor Morzik of KG.z.b.V.1 later recalled;

'In order to exploit fully the factor of surprise, it was of the utmost importance that the parachute troops be dropped over their respective targets simultaneously. The aircraft crossed the border zone at high altitude in order to keep out of the range of light AA and infantry fire. Once over the border, the formations descended at a previously ordered, uniformly decreasing speed to a lower altitude, approached the drop area at hedge-hopping altitude, climbed to the drop altitude of 120 m shortly before reaching the drop area, and then departed at hedge-hopping altitude. The return flight was carried out in the same fashion as the approach flight.'

It was a strange and worrying sight for the Dutch defenders on the ground at Waalhaven, one recounting how 'white dots suddenly appeared over the airfield like puffs of cotton wool. First, there were 20, then 50, then over 100 of them! And still they came popping out of the planes and beginning their low, oscillating descent. Then every machine gun opened up at the parachutes and at the planes. With so many targets the men just did not know where to aim.'

It took the paratroopers some 15-20 seconds to reach the ground once they left the Ju 52/3ms. Most landed in the assigned DZ, and so were able to engage the enemy quickly, including mounting an attack on the airport buildings where the Dutch commander had been celebrating his 40th birthday. However, one Junkers dropped its *Fallschirmjäger* directly amidst the burning hangars where aircraft ammunition and fuel was exploding, and many parachutes caught fire before the men touched down. Within a short time however, the Dutch defenders began surrendering, confused by the sight of green Very lights being fired by the Germans which they took to be a ceasefire order. Waalhaven airport was quickly taken by the *Fallschirmjäger* and the route to Rotterdam secured.

Elsewhere, south of the airport at Valkenburg, at 0456 hrs, five Ju 52/3ms dropped more sticks of paratroops from the six companies of FJR 2, and, just over 20 minutes later, with the field taken, they were reinforced by more Junkers bringing in air-landed *Fallschirmjäger*.

At Moerdijk, following an attack by Ju 87s intended to neutralise the bridge defences, the paratroops of II./FJR 1 were dropped from 53 Ju 52/3ms of Major Karl Georg Witt's I./KG.z.b.V.1 at 0500 hrs – the drops were made simultaneously at either end of the bridges in order to envelop the targets. A short, sharp engagement with Dutch forces ensued, but both the viaduct and the rail bridge were seized intact. In the more built-up area around Dordrecht, however, the paratroop force was limited to a single *Kompanie*, and ferried there by 12 Ju 52/3ms of 1./KG.z.b.V.172 under Hauptmann Rudolf Krause. The paratroop commander was killed in the fighting there when the Dutch launched a counter-attack and retook the bridge. Other German airborne units became locked in fierce combat around the town.

However, despite the pockets of tough resistance, the *Fallschirmjäger* managed to accomplish their mission and all the Dutch bridges remained intact. But this success had come at a heavy price for the Ju 52/3m crews. Nevertheless, a total of 4000 *Fallschirmjäger* had been dropped, as well as paratroop ammunition stock over Dordrecht. In its paratroop-dropping role, the Ju 52/3m had been crucial in the execution of German operations that concluded successfully in Holland on 14 May, just four days after their commencement.

The spartan interior of a Ju 52/3m *'Fallschirm und Luftlandetrupp-Flugzeug'* fitted out in Prague in 1941 for paratroop or air-landing operations. The fold-down seats are fitted with safety belts and the windows are curtained for nocturnal flights. The cable running along the roof may be the static line. The bulkhead wall with double doors leading to the cockpit has the stand-by and jump indicator lights, and the controls for heating and ventilation. Note the air vent in the fuselage roof

As far as the air-landing operations were concerned, with relatively few problems, the Ju 52/3m had proved that it could successfully tow laden gliders at night, in radio silence, in formation, using only visual navigation. Whilst the Germans capitalised on the success and publicity of the Eben-Emael raid, it would not have been possible without the quiet and professional contribution made by the Junkers and its crews to one of history's most audacious airborne raids.

However, other units did not fare so well in the attack on the Low Countries. Typical of the challenging operations that the *Transportflieger* undertook were those of KGr.z.b.V.9 on 10 May. That day, the *Gruppe* was tasked with ferrying troops from 22. *Infanterie-Division* (*Luftlande*) to nominated *Landeplätze* (landing grounds) around The Hague and Rotterdam, but ultimately its aircraft were forced to land variously on airfields, roads, beaches and in open countryside in the area. The 22. *Inf.-Div.*(*L.L.*) had been formed in Bremen in 1935 and over the following years trained up as a specialist air-landing unit. In the first days of May elements of the division's bicycle, motorcycle, infantry and signals units gathered on airfields around Lippspringe, from where the four *Staffeln* of KGr.z.b.V.9 were to fly them into Holland. KGr.z.b.V.9 was under the command of 44-year-old Major Johann Janzen, a highly experienced World War 1 aviator who had previously served as *Kommandeur* of IV./KGr.z.b.V.1.

A total of 54 Ju 52/3ms was available for the operation, including a specialist signals machine. Between 0555 hrs and 0626 hrs on the morning of 10 May, the aircraft took off from Lippspringe, but two Junkers experienced engine problems and were forced to abort. The remaining transports crossed the border in *Staffel* formations in broken cloud at 2000 m to be greeted by heavy AA fire over Rhenen and Culemborg, but the Dutch gunners failed to inflict any damage on the German aircraft.

Thirteen of the fifteen Ju 52/3ms of 1./KGr.z.b.V.9, carrying bicyclists, managed to land at the *Staffel*'s designated landing ground at *Landeplatz* II (Ockenburg) at 0745 hrs amidst strong enemy defensive fire and the wrecks of aircraft that had been destroyed in earlier air attacks. The situation was made worse by the soft ground of the coastal area around The Hague into which many Junkers of KGr.z.b.V.12, which had already set down over an hour earlier carrying other infantry elements of 22. *Inf.-Div.*(*L.L.*), had become bogged down. Consequently, Ockenburg was already littered with aircraft which blocked the runway when 1./KGr.z.b.V.9 arrived there. One of the *Staffel*'s Junkers overturned on landing and its tail broke off, while three others were so damaged by enemy shelling that they were written off.

Amidst such chaos, the aircrews and personnel of 22. *Inf.-Div.*(*L.L.*) battled to unload the Division's equipment under enemy infantry and artillery fire. As if that was not enough, Dutch bombers put in an appearance and destroyed four Junkers. Eventually, five aircraft were able to take off, carrying no fewer than 37 aircrew, many of those from aircraft left behind at Ockenburg. Four managed to return to Lippspringe, but one was hit by enemy ground fire near Wissel and had to make an emergency landing near Kleve.

Hauptmann Külbel led the aircraft of the *Stab*/KGr.z.b.V.9 towards *Landeplatz* III at Ypenburg. He recalled;

'I led the *Gruppenstab* around 0745 hrs over *Platz* III. Several burning Ju 52s [around eight] were on the field, but our own troops could not be seen. Our aircraft were shot at by heavy machine gun and rifle fire. Repeated attempts at landing were unsuccessful due to strong [enemy] fire. Some subsequent aircraft [possibly 9P+PB, 9P+EB and one aircraft from 2. *Staffel*] put down, but immediately went up in flames, while others were shot down as they prepared to land. During the mass attempt at landing the aircraft of the *Gruppenstab*, 2. and 3. *Staffeln* dispersed.

A Kette *of three Ju 52/3ms heads away as a cluster of paratroops lands on flat farmland in Holland in May 1940*

'Because the motorways were rendered useless for landing on by motor vehicles and concrete pipes located at regular intervals, I tried landing on *Platz* II, where I knew the majority of the landed troops were. Since this field was no longer viable because 1. *Staffel* had, meanwhile, landed there, I ended up landing with six aircraft from various *Staffeln* on a beach 1.5 km west of *Platz* II. I had earlier been ordered by radio to land on the coast. From there, three lightly damaged aircraft were able to take off after some weak and cowardly Dutch infantry [about one platoon] had been thrown back, leaving two dead. The remaining aircraft were unable to take off due either to bombardment or as a result of damage suffered during landing.'

The Ju 52/3ms of 2./KGr.z.b.V.9 crossed the Dutch/German border at 0730 hrs bound for *Landeplatz* III, but were fired at by AA guns west of Nijmegen, and any attempt at landing at Ypenburg proved impossible because of burning aircraft wrecks already on the ground as well as intense AA and machine gun fire from both sides. The *Staffel*'s cohesion was literally blown apart. One Junkers was hit by ground fire and shot down in flames, while the *Staffelkapitän* landed his aircraft on the motorway between The Hague and Rotterdam, two kilometres north of Delft. Another five Ju 52/3ms eventually landed on the road, some breaking up, others catching fire. Only the *Staffelkapitän* managed to take off again, his aircraft carrying his own crew, all unharmed, and six others.

Like 2. *Staffel*, 3./KGr.z.b.V.9 also became scattered as its aircraft searched for landing sites. Four Junkers managed to get down at, or near to, Ockenburg, while four landed on the motorway between Delft and The Hague, with two more coming down on the beach. Somehow, despite its tyres being shot through, Ju 52/3m 9P+BL managed to get airborne and returned from Ockenburg, but two aircraft went missing on the approach flight. Aircrew of the *Staffel* reported seeing the *Staffelkapitän*'s aeroplane take off from Ockenburg with a damaged tailwheel shortly after – it too went missing.

4./KGr.z.b.V.9 fared marginally better, as five of its Junkers landed on ground some 1.5 km southeast of *Landeplatz* III at Ypenburg and four on the motorway south of Delft. Although one aircraft returned to Lippspringe without landing, having been hit by AA fire, all others were unloaded. However, of the nine machines that landed, three were damaged and were abandoned. The crew of one of these aircraft survived, as did the wounded

Having uncoupled their parachutes, paratroop riflemen and a machine gun section quickly race for cover moments after reaching the ground. The man to the far right is probably the section leader, while in the centre another man carries the ammunition box for the 7.92 mm MG 34 machine gun being carried by his comrades, together with the tripod mount, to the left of the photograph

This Ju 52/3m has overshot the runway and lies perilously close to a road and pylon in France in 1940. The right-hand engine unit has buckled and a mainwheel appears to be laying in the ditch, but the aircraft will be salvageable

pilot of another, but the remaining crew members were reported missing. One Junkers crashed in a street in The Hague, with all on board killed. Documents recovered from the wreckage revealed a plan to capture the Dutch Royal Family.

Of the 53 Ju 52/3ms of KGr.z.b.V.9 that flew the operation, 43 were eventually unloaded in the area of The Hague, but the *Gruppe*'s losses and damage were catastrophic. Ten Junkers were thought to have been destroyed at, or around, Ypenburg, another went missing shortly after its return takeoff, one made an emergency landing during its return flight and 28 machines were damaged around The Hague.

Testimony to the remarkable resilience of the Ju 52/3m and its crews, once the surviving aircraft from the morning's mission had returned, so they were refuelled and reloaded in readiness for two further missions that day. At 1435 hrs eight aircraft took off from Lippspringe in two *Schwärme* lead by Hauptmann Külbel and Hauptmann Otto Heinrich Wildau, the *Gruppe* adjutant. Their task was to fly 70 men of *Infanterie-Regiment* 65, together with four field guns. This time orders had been issued at *Fliegerkorps* level that aircraft were not to land at fields that were not held securely in German hands, and so because *Landeplätze* II and III were still under intense fire, landing took place at *Platz* IV (Waalhaven). One Ju 52/3m, 9P+BH, was shot down in flames, but the remaining aircraft managed to unload safely on the northeastern edge of the field. All aircraft returned to Lippspringe between 1830 and 1845 hrs without further incident.

Meanwhile, at 1645 hrs, a third formation of six Ju 52/3ms under the command of Hauptmann Joachim Blechschmidt was assigned to ferry a squad of assault troops to Valkenburg, which, according to reports from the staff of the 22. *Inf.-Div.(L.L.)*, was in German hands. This was not actually the case, although a large Swastika had been laid out over the ground. As the Junkers approached, they were 'welcomed' by intense ground fire, and this, together with the fact that there was so much wreckage littering the surface of the field, meant that a landing was impossible. At that point, one Ju 52/3m split away from the formation and managed to land on the beach at Ockenburg, where friendly troops were observed. However, because of a lack of space, the remaining five aircraft were unable to land. Fortunately, losses did not materialise and all aircraft had returned to Lippspringe by 2050 hrs.

For the Ju 52/3m *Gruppen* operating that day there had been a heavy price to pay. At *Landeplatz* I (Valkenburg), I./KGr.z.b.V.172 under

Hauptmann Rudolf Krause sent 11 transports to drop 148 *Fallschirmjäger* – one was shot down before reaching the target, another was posted missing and a third damaged during the return flight. A force of 53 Ju 52/3ms from Hauptmann Hans-Eberhard Freiherr von Hornbach's KGr.z.b.V.11 based at Lippstadt flew nearly 800 air-landing troops to Valkenburg, losing just one aircraft shot down, but none of its machines returned, most being wrecked on landing. Another 37 Junkers of I./KG.z.b.V.1 headed for Valkenburg, but two were shot down on the approach flight and a third crashed while landing. Of the remaining machines, 20 had to return to base with troops still aboard, having been unable to land.

At *Landeplatz* II (Ockenburg), a Ju 52/3m of Hauptmann Theodor Beckmann's IV./KG.z.b.V.1 based at Loddenheide was lost before it reached the DZ for the *Fallschirmjäger* it was carrying, and 13 other aircraft from the *Gruppe* missed it altogether – 148 paratroops landed way off mark. Seventeen Junkers belonging to Oberstleutnant Gustav Wilke's I./KGr.z.b.V.12 flew in 221 troops from 22. *Inf.-Div.(L.L.)*, but lost seven aircraft as write-offs during the landing, with a further two badly damaged and seven less so and repairable.

Another 40 Ju 52/3ms from Beckmann's IV./KG.z.b.V.1 dropped *Fallschirmjäger* at *Landeplatz* III (Ypenburg) but lost one transport prior to the target. By the time the aircraft from this force returned home, 18 were found to be unserviceable because of damage inflicted by ground fire and two crash-landed. Another wave of 36 Junkers belonging to I./KGr.z.b.V.12 flew 429 troops of 22. *Inf.-Div.(L.L.)* to Ypenburg, but the mission proved nothing short of a disaster when 13 aircraft fell victim to ground fire, the remainder being forced to look for alternative landing sites.

As daylight broke over *Landeplatz* IV (Waalhaven), a formation of 53 Ju 52/3ms of Major Drewes' II./KG.z.b.V.1 based at Loddenheide appeared in the wake of a bombing run by He 111s of KG 4. The mission went relatively well, with just one Junkers crash-landing on return to base.

As described, the day's operations had also taken a heavy toll on KGr.z.b.V.9. One officer and five other ranks had been killed, another six officers and 66 other ranks were posted missing and one officer and ten other ranks wounded. And yet there was to be no respite for the crews of KGr.z.b.V.9, for the next day, 11 May, the *Gruppe* was assigned to fly two missions to Waalhaven. The first, involving one *Staffel* of 12 Ju 52/3ms under the leadership of Hauptmann Wildau, was to ferry in the staff of *Infanterie-Regiment* 72 on a course Lippspringe–Kleve–Moerdijk–Waalhaven. The Junkers took off at 1330 hrs and landed at *Landeplatz* IV at 1520 hrs. It took ten minutes for the men aboard to disembark and the aircraft to turn around for takeoff. They had returned to Lippspringe by 1650 hrs, refreshingly without loss, despite running into ground fire a few kilometres southeast of the landing site.

The second mission saw two *Staffeln*, comprising a total of 24 Ju 52/3ms under the respective commands of Hauptmann Külbel and Hauptmann Blechschmidt, take off at 1710 hrs to fly the same course to Waalhaven to ferry in the staff of *Infanterie-Regiment* 65 and a rifle company. One aircraft had to turn back with damage, but the remaining 23 landed without incident. It took 40 minutes to unload the Wehrmacht personnel, and all aircraft had returned to Lippspringe by 2130 hrs.

However, with so many of its Ju 52/3ms destroyed or damaged, and with its crews having suffered such heavy losses, the *Gruppe* was removed from any further involvement in the campaign. It would not be fully reinstated with aircraft until July, when it commenced flying routine transport missions to France and Belgium in support of the Luftwaffe's air operations against the British Isles.

A total of 242 German transport aircraft were listed as lost to all causes between April and June 1940, and it can be assumed that the bulk of these were Ju 52/3ms.

As part of a process of consolidation, in June 1940 the Fuhlsbüttel-based KGr.z.b.V.107, a part of X. *Fliegerkorps*, turned over half of its personnel and aircraft to KGr.z.b.V.108, which was based at Rantum and Hörnum at the time, but which soon moved north to Oslo-Fornebu, where its mixed bag of Ju 52/3ms (some float-equipped), He 111s and Fi 156 operated as part of *Luftflotte* 5.

In August 1940, elements of KG.z.b.V.1 and KG.z.b.V.2 were moved to France in preparation for *Unternehmen Seelöwe* (Operation *Sea Lion*), the planned invasion of England, but when this was cancelled, both *Geschwader* were called back to the Reich to assist with further training and to stand by for new tasks.

Nevertheless, despite the enormity of the tasks asked of it, and the operational losses suffered as a result, the Ju 52/3m had by the end of 1940 gained a reputation for being a mechanically reliable military aircraft. Its pilots and crews, often unsung, had demonstrated considerable skill and fortitude in their missions. These crews thought highly of the aircraft they came to know as the '*Tante Ju*'. However, just three Ju 52/3m pilots were awarded the Knight's Cross in 1940.

The first was Hauptmann Peter Ingenhoven of KGr.z.b.V.106, a *Gruppe* which in mid-1940 had been based in the Dortmund area. Ingenhoven was born on 16 December 1894, and in 1937 he joined KGr.z.b.V.1 at its formation at Fürstenwalde under Major Dr. Max Ziervogel. On 9 April he joined KGr.z.b.V.103 at Schleswig and was awarded the Knight's Cross for his service over Norway and while acting *Kommandeur* on 11 May after the death of Hauptmann Richard Wagner in action over Oslo the previous month. Shortly thereafter Ingenhoven was made *Staffelkapitän* of 3./KGr.z.b.V.106. In August 1941 he was promoted to Major and became commander of I./*Luftlandegeschwader* 1, where he oversaw Ju 52/3m–DFS 230 towing and air-landing operations in the Balkans. In December of that year Ingenhoven took command of KGr.z.b.V.900, but on 1 February 1942 his Ju 52/3m was shot down in the Beljevo-Velizh area, northeast of Vitebsk, and he was killed.

Thirteen days after Ingenhoven was awarded the Knight's Cross, Oberst Dipl.-Ing. Gerhard Conrad became a recipient. Conrad was born on 21 April 1895 at Pregelmühle bei Alsleben. He served as an infantry soldier during World War 1, rising to the rank of Leutnant. Conrad enjoyed exemplary service, but was wounded in action in March 1918 and was awarded several notable decorations, as well as being recommended for the *Pour le Mérite*. After inter-war service in the *Reichswehr*, he transferred to the Luftwaffe in 1935 and was appointed *Staffelkapitän* of 7./KG 152 in April 1936, then *Kommandeur* of I./KG 257 on the same date the

Troops wait to board Ju 52/3m 1Z+EK of 2./KG.z.b.V.1, possibly in France in 1941, in order to transfer to the Mediterranean. The aircraft carries the white Mediterranean theatre fuselage band

following year. In April 1938 Conrad took acting command of the Ju 52/3m-equipped I./KG.z.b.V.2 until the arrival of Hauptmann Hans-Eberhard von Hornstein in August, at which point he took over the leadership of the parent KG.z.b.V. 2. In July 1940, Conrad was posted to command the He 111-equipped KG 27, but after just three months he was appointed successively, as *Chef der Luftwaffe-Kontroll-Kommission* III, to the Staff of XI. *Fliegerkorps* and *Luftflottenkommando* 4 and various regional defence inspectorates. He passed into American captivity on 20 April 1945.

The third recipient was Gustav Wilke, born on 6 March 1898 at Deutsch Eylau in East Prussia. He joined the German Army in December 1916 and, like Conrad, fought in the infantry as a Leutnant. Between the wars he served in the *Reichswehr*, but transferred to the Luftwaffe in 1935 with the rank of Hauptmann. From October 1936, Wilke served in various training capacities before being appointed *Gruppenkommandeur* in the *Luftlandegeschwader Hagenow/Lippstadt* on 1 April 1939. He was promoted to Oberstleutnant and in April 1940 was appointed *Kommandeur* of KGr.z.b.V.12 and then of *Luftlandegeschwader* 1 until August 1941. He was awarded the Knight's Cross on 25 September 1940, the same day as Gerhard Conrad. From September 1941 Wilke was appointed as a special representative of the Luftwaffe with the Messerschmitt company to monitor the manufacture and development of large-capacity gliders. From March 1942 he served as commander of Luftwaffe field and *Fallschirmjäger* regiments and divisions. Wilke was made a Generalleutnant in August 1944, but was captured at Iglau on 5 May 1945.

To assess the value of the Ju 52/3m in 1940, one simply has to consider its role as a transporter of air-landed troops and materiel, as well as paratroops, and then to place a value on those troops within the context of German military aims. The seizure of key points in Norway and Denmark, and the capture of Eben-Emael, would not have happened – or at least perhaps not so efficiently – without the oft-overlooked means of delivering men and equipment to them. In this respect, arguably, the Ju 52/3m was as important as the crack troops and the successes themselves.

However, as the horizon of German war aims expanded in 1941 towards theatres of vast space and extreme climates, so there would be further demands placed on the production of Ju 52/3ms, as well as on maintenance and crews. The 'easy' times were over. The tests were coming.

A wounded or injured seaman is stretchered aboard a Ju 52/3m air ambulance, possibly D-VDZA of *Sanitätsflugbereitschaft* 11, in northern Germany in 1940, accompanied by a naval officer. The aircraft has been finished in white overall, with areas of black around the nose and engines. Black code letters are visible on the fuselage and left wing. During the winter of 1939-40, *Sanitätsflugbereitschaft* 11 flew supply missions from Norderney to isolated islands in the North Sea

CHAPTER SIX

POWDER KEG

This Ju 52/3m is believed to have been used as a transport by a *Staffel* of St.G 2 'Immelmann' during the early phase of the Balkan campaign. The emblem on the Junkers' nose resembles that of the 'Jesau' crusader's cross on a white shield, while the fuselage band was probably in the same shade of yellow as the theatre identity colour

By the spring 1941, much of Europe lay under the control of the Third Reich. In the East, most of Poland had been conquered, while to the West, the occupation of Norway, Denmark, the Netherlands, Belgium and France ensured that Germany controlled the western European coastline. Spain was neutral, but Franco's government was friendly to the Nazis, while Italy was now formally an ally in the Tripartite Pact. Great Britain alone stood as a belligerent opponent. To the southeast, the Balkan nations of Hungary, Rumania and Bulgaria had also joined the Pact, assuring Hitler of further Allies, and thus calm, in the region. This was important, for as the prospect of a vast military undertaking in the East grew ever closer, Hitler and the German High Command had been drawn to deal with what they perceived as an uncertain situation in the Balkans.

To see through its military endeavours and to fuel an ever-expanding Reich, Germany needed Rumanian oil. In late 1940, the Rumanian oilfields were relatively secure – they were beyond the range of the nearest British aircraft based in Palestine and Egypt. But if Britain decided to escalate its military presence in Greece, then Italy would be forced to fight for its occupation of that country, and, to the Germans, judging by Italy's recent record in North Africa, that could be questionable. The Germans were further helped on 25 March 1941 when the Yugoslavian Regent, Prince Paul, also signed the Tripartite Pact, thus placing his country under German influence.

On 13 December 1940 Hitler had issued a directive for what was codenamed Operation *Marita* in which he foresaw a German occupation of Greece in order to prevent the 'establishment of an air base which would threaten Italy in the first place, and, incidentally, the Rumanian oil fields'. These, in the context of Hitler's longer-term grand strategy, were high stakes.

But there had been a hiccup – and much to Hitler's consternation, it had been down to Italy. On 28 October 1940 the Italians had attacked Greece from Albania, Mussolini's reasoning founded, erroneously, on the belief that the Greeks would collapse and that the war would be concluded quickly. However, against fierce Greek opposition the Italians were soon forced to pull back into the mountains of Albania, where they lingered, while the Greeks made a foothold in the south of that country. The *Führer* was furious with the recklessness of *Il Duce* for it provided Britain with a reason to intervene and also raised Soviet suspicion, since Moscow was eyeing Bulgaria as a potential satellite state.

Reluctantly, Hitler recognised that the Italians would have to be supported in their venture, but supplying their troops in Albania by sea from Italy would be dangerous because of the presence of enemy submarines in Albanian coastal waters. Furthermore, the Italians claimed that the *Regia Aeronautica*'s Savoia-Marchetti S.82 transports were not available because of commitments in the Mediterranean and Africa. This left the Luftwaffe, and, in late November 1940 III./KG.z.b.V.1, with a full complement of 53 Ju 52/3ms under the command of Hauptmann Rudolf Starke, who, before taking up his command had had considerable experience in leading blind-flying training courses, assembled at Wesendorf in readiness for operations in support of the Italians. Many of the *Gruppe*'s crews were veterans – and survivors – of operations over Norway and Holland and were thus among the best that could be offered. From Wesendorf, it was planned that the *Gruppe* would fly to Foggia in southeast Italy, staging via Graz. The Ju 52/3ms arrived at Wesendorf on 8 and 9 December, while the unit's ground personnel had already departed for Foggia by train.

III./KG.z.b.V.1's mission was to transport Italian specialist winter warfare troops as well as winter clothing, weapons, ammunition and support equipment, to a ratio of 40/60, across the Adriatic to an airfield in the Albanian capital of Tirana. Return flights would see the Ju 52/3ms bringing back wounded troops and unserviceable weapons and equipment. Organisationally, the *Gruppe* was assigned to the *General der Deutschen Luftwaffe beim Oberkommando der König Italienische Luftwaffe* (ITALUFT), Generalleutnant Ritter von Pohl, based in Rome, but operational orders would be routed on a day-to-day basis via the supply and logistics branches of the Italian High Command, to whom the *Gruppe* assigned its own liaison officer and interpreter.

Heavy equipment bound for units of the VIII. *Fliegerkorps* operating in the Balkans is manhandled aboard a Ju 52/3m at a supply base in Rumania or Bulgaria

The fact that Starke and many of his men had blind-flying experience was an important factor since bad weather and foggy conditions over Tirana were anticipated. However, it subsequently transpired that whenever Foggia became smothered by low-lying cloud, the pilots of the Ju 52/3ms would have to resort to extremely low altitude when approaching the airfield from the sea. From this perspective, it became apparent to the German crews that the airfields at Bari or Brindisi would have made better choices.

On the positive side, supply of fuel was plentiful at Foggia and there was no pressure to ferry a minimum tonnage per day since tonnage would depend very much on how many sorties the Junkers would be able to fly per day, allowing for loading and unloading, and weather. Furthermore, the air crews were reassured by the fact that the servicing and maintenance of their aircraft was undertaken by their own groundcrews, while the Italians provided more than adequate numbers of men to handle the loading and unloading, and cooperation in this regard was good. In addition, there were good AA defences at Foggia and Tirana, and medical personnel and fleets of ambulances were available to take delivery of the incoming wounded at Foggia. All the Ju 52/3ms were fitted with life vests and inflatable rubber dinghies, and a *Regia Aeronautica* air-sea rescue unit was placed on readiness at Bari. For communications purposes, III./KG.z.b.V.1 also set up its own radio station at Foggia.

Once missions commenced, there was no interruption from enemy aircraft, either in the air during the 320-km flight to and from Tirana, or on the ground, with the exception of one RAF bombing raid on Foggia, which failed to inflict any damage. Formation flights were usually made in daylight in *Ketten* of three aircraft, each *Kette* taking off at five-minute intervals. During the first phase of operations up until mid-January 1941, the Ju 52/3ms achieved around 100 flights per day, reducing to approximately 60 during the final weeks of the operation, but there were ten days when adverse weather precluded any flying.

Over a total of 50 days of flying, III./KG.z.b.V.1 flew 4028 sorties to Tirana, of which 1665 were predominantly troop transport and 2363 were mainly for the ferrying of supplies. Altogether, 28,871 Italian soldiers were ferried to Albania along with 4700 tons of supplies, while some 10,941 personnel, of whom 8730 were wounded, were brought back to Italy. No aircraft were lost during the Tirana flights, which, while undertaken in conditions akin to peacetime, nevertheless provided invaluable experience for later Luftwaffe transport missions to and from North Africa.

In January 1941, in readiness for large-scale operations in the Balkans, the Luftwaffe's *Chef der Ausbildungswesen* (Chief of Training) formed three new Ju 52/3m-equipped *Gruppen* all based on airfields around Berlin – KGr.z.b.V.40 under the command of Major Ernst Deutsch, KGr.z.b.V.50 and KGr.z.b.V.60. Early the following months, three more *Gruppen* were established in the shape of KGr.z.b.V.101 (a re-formed unit), KGr.z.b.V.104 and KGr.z.b.V.105. The *Chef der Ausbildungswesen* placed all six of these units within the newly-formed XI. *Fliegerkorps* under the command of Generalleutnant Student at Berlin-Tempelhof, which was intended as a *Korps* headquarters for the replacement and training of *Fallschirmjäger*.

On 6 April 1941 Germany invaded Yugoslavia and Greece with speed and might, but on the periphery was Rumania, where the Germans had real fears that the Soviet Union might attempt an invasion in order to protect its own interests in the Balkans. If it did, the likelihood was that Rumanian forces would be unable to hold back such an incursion. Under the German-Rumanian Treaty of 1939, Germany had sent military personnel to Rumania to assist in the development and training of the Rumanian Army. In addition, they were to organise sufficient defence for the Rumanian oil fields, which would be of paramount importance to Germany's future war aims.

It was against this scenario that the Ju 52/3m next found itself a pawn in a politico-strategic Balkan game. In addition to its movements in Yugoslavia and Greece, it became essential that Germany dispatch a large military force to Rumania that would hopefully demonstrate to the Russians at best the degree to which protection of Rumania was held in Berlin or, at worst, to resist any initial Soviet attack long enough to move in reinforcements to the country. The challenge was getting these forces to Rumania quickly. No safe direct overland route existed. Routing via Hungary would have introduced slow diplomatic negotiations, and any move through Yugoslavia at that point was impossible because the outcome of German military operations was still uncertain at such an early stage. Once again, air transport seemed to be the key and, fortunately, the Hungarian government offered no objection to Luftwaffe aircraft routing over its territory.

So it was that from late March 1941, the *Gruppen* of Oberst Morzik's KG.z.b.V.1 and Oberst Rüdiger von Heyking's KG.z.b.V.2 assembled on airfields in the Wiener-Neustadt area in order to prepare to receive the troops and equipment of the 22. *Luftlande-Infanterie Division*. Shortly after, elements of the division arrived and were assigned for airlift amongst the various *Gruppen*. Throughout 6 April the Ju 52/3ms took off in large formations carrying the men, equipment and light weapons of the division bound for Bucharest and Ploesti, where they would be used as 'security forces'. The flights were scheduled to arrive at pre-determined times to facilitate smooth and efficient unloading.

However, while on course over the Leitha and southern Carpathian mountains, inclement weather forced down several Ju 52/3ms. These losses were mainly aircraft flown by less experienced pilots, but were judged by Luftwaffe commanders to be commensurate with the importance of the operation. By far the bulk of 22. *Inf.-Div.(L.L.)*'s forces were landed safely. In a post-war account, Friedrich-Wilhelm Morzik commented;

'This airlift was motivated by both political and strategic considerations, and it shows clearly the advantages of having an air transport force ready for action at all times. Air transport was the only possible method of accomplishing this action rapidly and successfully. Since it was neither part of an offensive action nor an integral component of an operation already underway, but rather a preventative measure, it differs from all other undertakings of the same general type.'

By 13 April advancing German forces had taken Belgrade, the Yugoslavian government having been deposed by a military coup in late March. The ground plan for *Marita* hinged around offensive operations

Air-drop canisters containing equipment for German paratroop units are relayed from a truck to waiting Ju 52/3ms. While in the Balkans, Junkers transports would fly through bad weather, over mountains, frequently on several sorties per day, in order to fly *Fallschirmjäger* and supplies to key targets and forward airfields. Note the corrugated metal shock absorbers for the canisters and the triangular tactical marking on the rudder of the Ju 52/3m in the background. These Ju 52/3ms have had yellow paint applied to engine cowlings, wingtips and rudders as a theatre identification marking

conducted by 2. *Armee* and 12. *Armee*. These armies were supported in their attack by the strike units of *Luftflotte* 4, which in turn depended on nine air transport *Gruppen* to support them. Aside from I. and II./KG.z.b.V.1 and KG.z.b.V.2, the other Ju 52/3m units assigned to *Marita* were KGr.z.b.V.60, under Major Walter Hammer, a *Gruppe* that had been formed in the Berlin area in January 1941 before moving to Wien, and KGr.z.b.V.102, under the recently appointed Major Walter Erdmann, who had previously been on the staff of the *Grosse Kampffliegerschule* at Tutow. As noted earlier, this unit had been re-formed in Berlin as recently as February 1941, having been partially disbanded in May of the previous year and its Ju 52/3ms dispersed among training units. It was the same for KGr.z.b.V.101 under Oberstleutnant Ernst Mundt, who had also served at the Gr.Kfl.Sch.Tutow.

Finally, the three *Gruppen* of Major Rudolf Krause's KGr.z.b.V.172, which had also been formed in the Berlin area, were slated for the Balkans. These units, which numbered some 270 Ju 52/3ms and were all at full strength, and stiffened by crews with experience gained over Norway and Holland, had been assigned to 7. *Fliegerdivision* for operational control.

Egon Kieffer, a war correspondent, reported from the Balkans that, 'the performance of the Ju 52 transports ensured the operations of the Stukas and fighters – daily their crews flew for more than ten hours'. Kieffer was assigned to one of the Ju 52/3m *Gruppen* supporting VIII. *Fliegerkorps*, von Richthofen's specialist Stuka and close-support *Korps*. He described the conditions facing the *Transportflieger* in the Balkans;

'More than once in this Balkan campaign have the men of the groundcrews perched on empty bomb crates at the edge of airfields and stared longingly out at the sky hoping that a good old "Ju" would approach over the snow-coated crests of the mountains to re-supply them with bombs and fuel. For more than in any other campaign, the Stuka and fighter units of our *Korps* in the Balkans have depended on transport aircraft for supplies. The huge distances between the supply bases and the airfields of the close-support units mean that a regular and timely supply of the most urgently needed materiel, bombs and fuel is impossible by land.

'In these days of relentless advances, in which each operation can be planned at the last minute, the men of the *Transportgruppen* assigned to our *Korps* have accomplished the maximum aeronautical performance through expending tireless physical effort. For weeks on end the transport crews have operated every day for ten hours at a time over the wild and craggy mountains of the Balkans. The average daily run has been over 2000 km, which the crews have flown selflessly. Tackling vast distances, through driving snow and ice, and under the most difficult weather conditions, the crews have acquired a tenacious reputation. Often the men of these units are fired upon by scattered enemy divisions during their flights across Serbia, and many have been hit by flak in the tail assembly or fuselage, forcing emergency landings, which, from examining the *Gruppe* war diary, do not always make happy reading. It is hard and strenuous work, demanding the crews of the *Gruppe* from dawn until late into the evening.

'During the days of February and March, because rain and snow had softened the hastily prepared airfields in Bulgaria, takeoff and landing with their machines loaded to the maximum limits was often an aeronautical feat. On one occasion, there was an overnight snowfall of half-a-metre, and all aircraft had sunk into it. Despite this, the *Korps* Quartermaster gave the order that all machines still operational were to be ready for takeoff. Without hesitation, the *Gruppenkommandeur* arranged to have 12 m-long planks of wood placed before each machine. With difficulty, the "Jus" then took off from the planks. At full speed the aircraft went over them, and finally got off the ground in pairs.

'But it is precisely as a result of these difficulties, and overcoming them, that the men of the *Gruppe* experience some all too rare cheer. Most of them are looking forward to making course for new airfields, which have been set up very close to the front. The supply men will then get an impression of combat operations – something which can easily be lost in lengthy flights elsewhere.

'The performance of this *Gruppe* in replenishing supplies made it an irreplaceable part of our flying operations in the southeastern theatre of war. In the Balkans alone, the machines of this *Gruppe* have covered 1,952,360 km, which is the equivalent of 50 times the Earth's circumference. They carried 517,150 kg of bombs and 1,810,350 kg of other supplies from the supply depots to the front. There were a further 1,674,400 litres of fuel and oil. Some 50 railway freight wagons would have been required just to move the bombs. But such transport in Greece and also in Serbia is an illusory prospect, since all the railway bridges are in ruins and the railway network has been destroyed in many places.

'These transport aircraft became especially valuable when there was a need for a sudden advance against Serbia. Within three days 7320 men from the ground forces were lifted from various parts of Bulgaria to the Bulgarian-Yugoslavian border. They were the few, tireless carriers who helped to facilitate the rapid and successful implementation of the Balkan campaign.'

As the Wehrmacht advanced through Greece supported by the Luftwaffe, German planners recognised that a potential stumbling block to their war aims would be the Corinth Canal, which ran between, and separated, the Peloponnese and the mainland of central Greece. As they pulled back, British and Commonwealth forces in Greece, numbering some 50,000 men, would strengthen their defence of the Isthmus of Corinth using the waterway as a line of defence with which to block off the Peloponnese. Thus a plan was devised to once again mount a swift airborne operation to seize the only bridge across the canal to allow German forces to maintain the momentum of their advance.

On 25 April, German ground forces moved forward from Molos, driving south. The British commanders realised that a German attempt to take the Isthmus of Corinth would threaten their planned evacuation of Australian and New Zealand units from the beaches at Argos and Kalamata.

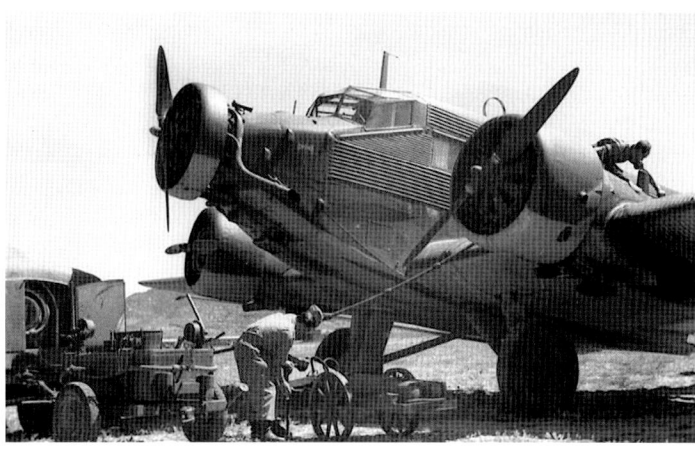

This Ju 52/3m is being refuelled from a bowser at an airfield in Greece. This would be a welcome facility for the groundcrews, who were frequently forced to rely on hand pumps at forward airfields in the Balkans

Meanwhile, most of *Fallschirmjägeregiment* 2, totalling just over 2000 men, was tasked with conducting an assault on the Isthmus and occupying both sides of the canal. In an operation that bore similarities to those conducted in Holland, the paratroops were to overwhelm enemy resistance and then to hold the bridge and the canal until the arrival of ground forces. They would be flown to their target by the Ju 52/3ms of a composite group formed from I. and II./KG.z.b.V.2, I./KG.z.b.V.1, KGr.z.b.V.60, KGr.z.b.V.102 and I./*Luftlandegeschwader* 1, and under the overall operational control of KG.z.b.V.2, led by Oberst von Heyking.

In order to maintain secrecy, the plan was for the Ju 52/3ms to fly the mission from Plovdiv in Bulgaria. From Wiener Neustadt, the aircraft would make an interim refuelling stop at Larissa in Thessaly, Greece, on the 25th, the night before the operation was due to take place. At Plovdiv, the *Fallschirmjäger* carefully loaded the aircraft with their equipment. The move from Plovdiv to Larissa was planned with precision to avoid enemy detection, with the first aircraft arriving there at dusk. Most of the Ju 52/3ms made the trip singly or in small formations, and, despite the fact that some individual *Gruppen* were unable to maintain cohesion as darkness approached, by nightfall, all aircraft had landed safely.

However, the 'loose' and extended takeoff from Plovdiv of such a large number of aircraft inevitably resulted in some organisational difficulties at Larissa, which was already home to Luftwaffe fighter and Ju 87 units. In the darkness 'misplaced' aircraft had to be moved to areas where their units were parked on an airfield that was already overcrowded and lacked sufficient ground and servicing facilities, while refuelling took the whole night since the fuel was provided from a central area by means of hand-pumping from drums! The assembled *Gruppen* were at least fortunate enough not to have to suffer enemy air attack – the results of which could have been catastrophic.

Also preparing for operations were the Ju 52/3m–DFS 230 *Schleppzüge* (glider tow) combinations of I./LLG 1 under Major Stein. These combinations would carry the para-engineers who would seize the ends of the canal bridge and deactivate any explosive charges that the British may have laid. The unit's glider crews and groundcrews had departed their base at Hildesheim by train on 20 April, routing via Regensburg and ultimately to Plovdiv. Around 15-20 disassembled gliders also arrived by train and were re-assembled in the hangars before being anchored down in the open. On the 25th, six *Schleppzüge* took off bound for the interim landing ground of Larissa, a distance of 350 km. The Ju 52/3ms released their gliders and then landed. The gliders were dispersed to the edge of the airfield. At 2200 hrs, more Ju 52/3ms arrived carrying the para-engineers, while another brought in aerial images of the target for study.

Two hours before dawn on the 26th, the commander of British forces in Greece, Gen Maitland Wilson, crossed the bridge over the Corinth Canal, having evacuated his headquarters in Athens. He was fortunate. By daybreak, all the paratroop-carrying and tow Junkers had been refuelled and were ready for their missions, the paratroop-carriers each loaded with 12 men plus weapons, munitions and limited supplies.

At 0500 hrs, amidst clouds of dust, six Ju 52/3m–DFS 230 tow combinations of I./LLG 1 took off from Larissa in two *Ketten* on the

220-km run to Corinth. The swirling dust forced the Junkers pilots to make blind starts, and it was not until the combinations in the first *Kette* to take off had reached an altitude of around 50-80 m that the pilots of the gliders were able to make out the Ju 52/3ms in front of them. The second *Kette* had to attain 100 m before they were clear of the dust. Once airborne, the entire formation turned in a wide circle, with the snow-covered Mount Olympus glistening in the rays of the rising sun in the distance off to starboard. However, in the thin air over the mountains, the tow Junkers struggled to climb, but eventually, 20 km from the target, the combinations successfully uncoupled.

Meanwhile, Ju 52/3ms heavily laden with *Fallschirmjäger* took off, on schedule, in three-aircraft *Ketten* and in cloud-threatened skies at 0500 hrs, climbing as quickly as they could and heading south. With each *Kette* close behind the one in front, they crossed the Pindus Mountains at 3000 m – a terrain bereft of any visible landmarks in the dawn light. As such the pilots relied both on carefully computed navigational data and the exhaust flames from the aircraft ahead of them. A war reporter was on board one of the Ju 52/3ms carrying *Fallschirmjäger* heading for the canal, and he experienced at first hand the excitement and the tension;

'In the early dawn we flew over the Greek countryside. We had known since the previous night the operation was on. The magic word for each *Fallschirmjäger* – operation. For almost a year we had been waiting for this day. This time, everything must work. Now, in *Kette* after *Kette* of our aircraft, with our 'chutes packed on our backs, the target firmly imprinted on us, we cannot be called back. The farewell to our comrades who would not be joining us and who had watched our preparations with disappointment in their eyes, was sombre. But we are on for it. Twelve men in our machine. A sworn group, each one knows precisely how to do his job. It's tightly packed in our aircraft because we are heavily loaded. "Just like a bunch of Santas", comments one of our comrades. Whatever there is to carry, we're carrying it. Especially weapons, ammunition and food. We still do not know how long it will take for the ground troops to relieve us. This flight is the last ordeal. The appearance of the magnificent mountain scenery below us is a welcome relief, since the opportunities for meaningful conversation are very limited against the noise of the engines.

'Most of us have to make do with our own thoughts. The premonition of a special experience is imprinted on all our faces. Our leader, an Oberleutnant, who will be the first to jump, maintains a cheerful disposition, which is wonderful, because it comes from the heart. He's an *Ostmärker* [Austrian], from around the Wörthersee, and tells us of how beautiful it is. The flight is taking long enough.'

Luftwaffe groundcrew members heave oil drums aboard a Ju 52/3m transport for ferrying to German ground forces in the Balkans. The generous size of the fuselage access hatch and the strength of the lower door hinges allowed for the handling of many different types of bulky and heavy items. As the drums of precious fuel are loaded on board, an NCO loadmaster supervises the process and keeps a count

Passing the Pindus, the Ju 52/3ms, now in a long column, three aircraft abreast, descended to 30 m above the water off Patrae. They then turned east-southeast towards the DZ at Corinth, concealed by their low altitude and the haze in the Gulf. As they climbed to 120 m, the *Fallschirmjäger* prepared themselves. As the war reportee described;

'Again and again, we peer ahead of us, as far as we can see. A magnificent view – *Kette* after *Kette*, *Staffel* after *Staffel* of our good old Ju 52/3ms, all on course towards our destination. Light comes as we reach the sea. Now it's just 15 minutes. A unique, indescribable tension grips us. There, ahead, lies our target, the entrance to the Corinth Canal. Also German aircraft on a reciprocal course, which have already dropped our comrades and who are now already in combat with the enemy.

'We prepare for the jump and make ourselves as comfortable as possible, ready for the jump order. The signal – a piercing sound that probably none of us will ever forget – sounds. Now, jump!'

Immediately ahead, the spearhead group from I./LLG 1 in three DFS 230 gliders had just landed the para-engineers who would secure the ends of the bridge. As well, Ju 87s of *General der Flieger* von Richthofen's VIII. *Fliegerkorps* bombed the roads around the canal. The arrival of the *Fallschirmjäger* jumping from their Ju 52/3ms amidst the bombing overwhelmed and confused the tired and ill-prepared British forces. Furthermore, one group of paratroopers from 3./FJR 2 jumped a few seconds early and landed in the sea. They drowned before they could be helped. One Ju 52/3m was lost when it failed to gain sufficient height to clear the mountains. Only two men managed to exit the aircraft. As von Richthofen noted in his diary;

'A parachute landing took place at 0630 hrs. Went off smoothly. Only a few losses. The canal and bridges are now in our hands intact. Hardly any losses. During the time our men were removing demolition charges from the bridge, it blew up sky high.'

Fortunately for the Germans, their glider-borne para-engineers were able to construct a temporary bridge relatively quickly.

The attack on the Isthmus of Corinth cut off all British troops north of the canal, including the entire 4th New Zealand Brigade and many other units making for the Peloponnese. The official British history records it, somewhat understatedly, as 'a day of uncertainty and rumour'. The Germans took 12,000 prisoners from both sides of the canal, while their own losses stood at 63 killed and 174 wounded or missing.

Having dropped the paratroops, the Ju 52/3ms turned back for Larissa, flying once again at low level along the same route as the approach flight. When they landed, they were made ready for a possible second run with another wave of *Fallschirmjäger* during the afternoon, but so successful had the operation been that this was not required. At that point, the Ju 52/3ms were withdrawn.

By early May, many of the Ju 52/3ms that had been engaged in carrying supplies and paratroops during the campaigns in Yugoslavia and Greece were badly in need of overhaul. They were sent back to Germany where, 'thanks to the ceaseless efforts of the workshops', they underwent maintenance and repair. A total of 324 transport aircraft were reported as lost to all causes between April and June 1941, a rise of 82 compared with the same months in 1940, and many of these, if not most, would have been Ju 52/3ms (this would have included those machines lost over Crete in May during Operation *Merkur* – not covered in this book).

At this time, some 15-20 Junkers were assigned to *Sonderkommando Junck*, the planned Luftwaffe detachment intended for operations in Iraq in support of the anti-British Prime Minister there, Rashid Ali al-Gaylani. Ultimately, however, even this small number of Junkers would be required for more pressing needs elsewhere. Nevertheless, al-Gaylani cut relationships with Britain and supported a mutiny within the Iraqi army. Britain then instigated economic sanctions. On 30 April, rebel Iraqi forces began a siege of the British base at Habbaniya. The British sent more troops from Egypt and India amidst concern that the supply of Iraqi oil could be in jeopardy. Meanwhile, al-Gaylani appealed to the German *Führer* for aid, to which he agreed, including a small number of Ju 52/3ms. These aircraft are believed to have been drawn from KGr.z.b.V.106 based at Insterburg, which formed a *Sonderkommando*/KGr.z.b.V.106 comprising as many as 20 Ju 52/3ms, which subsequently, and briefly, became known as the *Lufttransportstaffel Rother* after its commander, Hauptmann Harry Rother. The plan was to base the transports in Sicily, from where they would fly fuel and supplies into Syria and Iraq.

In addition to the Junkers, the *Sonderkommando* was to comprise – on paper – nine He 111s from II./KG 4, 14 Bf 110s from 4./ZG 76 and two Ju 90s. In reality, only a small number of the Ju 52/3ms went to Athens, where Iraqi markings were applied and from there the plan was to fly to Iraq, staging via Rhodes and Damascus to Baghdad, but little information was given to the crews about political events in the country. As far as is known, only two Ju 52/3ms eventually made it to Iraq, and one is believed to have been photographed at Mosul on 16 May.

However, when the *Sonderkommando* arrived at Mosul its personnel found that the siege of Habbaniya had dissipated and that the Iraqi Air Force had, to all intents and purposes, been neutralised. On 29 May, with his authority in question, and fearing a British onslaught on Baghdad, al-Gaylani fled Iraq for Persia. The same day, *Sonderkommando Junck* was forced to depart Iraq, leaving many of its aeroplanes abandoned and wrecked in the desert. One of the Ju 52/3ms was used to evacuate the groundcrew to Aleppo, in Syria.

Away from the periphery, there was to be little respite for the aircraft that had proved itself such a hardy, dogged and flexible 'jack of all trades' in Spain, then in the campaigns in Poland, Scandinavia, northwest Europe and in the Balkans. Hitler and his commanders had their eyes focused on new ambitions, as well as the need to secure areas where the German strategic position was threatened. The trusty 'old *Tante Ju*' would again play a vital role in these new ambitions and areas, which would stretch from Crete to North Africa and as far east as the Volga River, in the Soviet Union. But in doing so, the Ju 52/3m's hardiness and flexibility, and its crews, would be stretched to the limit by extreme climates and skies teeming with enemy aircraft. Ernst Zindel's design would have to prove itself once more.

One of the few Ju 52/3ms to be operated by *Sonderkommando Junck* in Iraq, this machine is believed to have been photographed at Mosul on 16 May 1941. It may have been an aircraft seconded from KGr.z.b.V.106, and had Iraqi markings applied

APPENDICES

APPENDIX 1

JUNKERS Ju 52/3m EARLY MILITARY VARIANTS

mg3e: *Behelfsbomber* (also transport and convertible as floatplane). Three x 660 hp BMW 132A engines. Three ESAC/250 vertical bomb cells in freight cabin for 6 x 250 kg or 24 x 50 kg bombs. Retractable ventral gun 'bin' and open dorsal machine-gun mount.

Wingspan:	29.25 m
Length:	18.90 m
Height:	6.10 m
Wing area:	110.5 m^2
Empty weight:	5900 kg
Total freight:	4100 kg
Flying weight:	10,000 kg
Wing loading:	90.5 kg/m^2
Power loading:	5.06 kg/hp
Power/wing area loading:	17.9 hp/m^2
Maximum speed:	300 km/h
Maximum cruising at 2500 m:	283 km/h
Economical cruising at 2500 m:	270 km/h
Landing speed:	104 km/h
Range at cruising speed:	1500 km
Climb to 1000 m:	4.1 min
Climb to 3000 m:	14.5 min
Ceiling:	6600 m

mg4e: Transport. Three x 660 hp BMW 132A or T engines. Strengthened floor, large loading doors on starboard side and roof. Internal steel fixing points. Strengthened landing gear.

Seven *Ausführung* (type variants):
E – *Kisten-Transportflugzeug* (general transport/crates etc.)
F – *Fallschirmschützen- und Luftlandetrupp-Flugzeug* (Paratroop and air-landing)
H – *Hörsaal-Flugzeug* (instruction/classroom aircraft)
R – *Reise-Flugzeug* (courier and liaison aircraft)
S – *Sanitätsflugzeuge* (air ambulance)
St – *Staffeltruppentransport-Flugzeug* (*Staffel*/unit-level transport)
Plus window mounts could be added as a seventh option for all types except 'S'.

APPENDIX 2

ORGANISATIONAL STRUCTURE OF A *KAMPFGRUPPE ZUR BESONDEREN VERWENDUNG* (BOMBER GROUP FOR SPECIAL PURPOSES)

Stabsschwarm (Staff Flight) – five Ju 52/3m and one Bf 108 liaison aircraft

Staff – *Kommandeur*
Adjutant, Technical Officer, Signals Officer, Motor Officer,
Administration Officer, Medical Officer,
Clerks, Drivers, Typists, Orderlies
Five aircrews
(one aircrew – pilot, flight mechanic, radio operator, gunner and jump master for paratroop operations)

1. *Staffel* (Squadron) – 12 x Ju 52/3m
2. *Staffel* – 12 x Ju 52/3m
3. *Staffel* – 12 x Ju 52/3m
4. *Staffel* – 12 x Ju 52/3m

In total – 53 Ju 52/3m (including six with *Stab*)

Each *Staffel* included 12 Aircrews, Hauptfeldwebel (senior NCO), Clerk, Workshop Foreman, Senior Armourer, Radio Operator, Drivers

Fliegerhorst Betriebskompanie (Airfield Maintenance Company)

1. *Betriebszüge* (Section)
For engines, fuselage, landing gear
2. *Betriebszüge*
3. *Betriebszüge*
4. *Betriebszüge*
Wartungszug (Workshop Section)

ORGANISATIONAL STRUCTURE OF A *KAMPFGESCHWADER ZUR BESONDEREN VERWENDUNG* (BOMBER WING FOR SPECIAL PURPOSES)

Stab (Staff) – one Ju 52/3m and one Bf 108 liaison aircraft
Operations Officer (Ia) – Adjutant, Technical Officer, Signals Officer, Medical Officer

I. *Gruppe* (Group) – 53 Ju 52/3m and *Fliegerhorst Betriebskompanie*
II. *Gruppe* – 53 Ju 52/3m and *Fliegerhorst Betriebskompanie*
III. *Gruppe* – 53 Ju 52/3m and *Fliegerhorst Betriebskompanie*

IV. *Gruppe** – 53 Ju 52/3m and *Fliegerhorst Betriebskompanie*

In total – 213 Ju 52/3m
*When no IV. *Gruppe*, strength = 159 Ju 52/3m

Total strength – 160 Ju 52/3m (including *Stab* machine) and one Bf 108

COLOUR PLATES

1
Ju 52/3m Wk-Nr 4009 CB-18 *HUANUNI* of the *Fuerza Aérea Boliviana*, Bolivia, 1933

Wk-Nr 4009 was one of three Ju 52/3ms that saw service with the FAB in 1933 during the Chaco War between Bolivia and Paraguay. Having arrived in South America, the FAB painted the aircraft in a dark green base, over which was applied a mottle of lighter green and brown. The Junkers bore its name on at least the left side of its fuselage and the Bolivian colours were applied to wing surfaces and the rudder. Owing to regular use, operating conditions and climate, these aircraft quickly took on a worn appearance.

2
Ju 52/3m Wk-Nr 5020 D-AZIS *HORST WESSEL* of the *Regierungsstaffel*, 1935

D-AZIS was the transport aircraft of the SA *Stabschef* (Chief of Staff), Obergruppenführer Viktor Lutze, during the late 1930s. The unique overall brown colour of the aircraft was probably intended to be representative of the 'brownshirts', and the emblem on the wings was that of the *Sturmabteilung* ('SA'). The tail was adorned in the standard red band with *Hakenkreuz* for the period, with the name of the aircraft painted in the usual DLH style along the forward fuselage.

3
Ju 52/3m 27+E11 of 1./KG 753, Gotha, late 1935

This aircraft was finished in overall RLM 63 hellgrau (light grey), with nose, engine cowlings and wheel spats in black, and with the stretched diamond pattern on the spats in white. The fuselage code was in black and the tailplane national marking is the black/white/red early style, which originated from 6 July 1933. The aircraft carries the five-digit, alpha-numeric fuselage code, with the second digit denoting the first number of the unit designation. *Balkenkreuz* is early style.

4
Ju 52/3mg3e S7+L15 of *Fliegergruppe* (S) or *Grosse Kampffliegerschule Lechfeld*, Lechfeld, 1935-38

A typical Ju 52/3m of a pre-war bomber training unit during the late 1930s. The aircraft is finished in overall hellgrau (RLM 63), with nose, engine cowlings and wheel spats in black, and with the stretched diamond pattern on the spats in white. The fuselage cross is in the early style. The fuselage code was in black and the tail unit was adorned in the standard red, white and black *Hakenkreuz* marking.

5
Ju 52/3m 42+C30 of II./KG 254, Eschwege or Giessen, 1937

Finished in overall RLM 63 hellgrau, this *Behelfsbomber* was probably used as a trainer for crews of II./KG 254. It might have been a former DLH machine because it carried wide black stripes on its upper wing surfaces. The engine cowlings and wheel spats were in black, the *Balkenkreuz* in the pre-war style, and the two, bright white fuselage stripes were probably intended as an aid to airborne recognition.

6
Ju 52/3m 01+14 of KGr.z.b.V.1, Wyk auf Föhr, early 1939

This worn-looking aircraft retains the pre-1938 style splinter pattern of a base of RLM 63 hellgrau overlaid with areas of 61 dunkelbraun and 62 grün. The last two digits of the code appear faded. The significance of the black disc forward of the code is not known for certain, but may have been for formation training purposes.

7
Ju 52/3m 21+H12 of 2./KG 152, Neubrandenburg, 1937

This Junkers bomber was finished in a strong splinter pattern of RLM 63 hellgrau/61 dunkelbraun/62 grün. The *Balkenkreuz* is in the period style, but has no black outline. The tail *Hakenkreuz* was applied mid-position over the join between the tail and rudder. The code denotes the second *Geschwader* (2) formed within Luftkreiskommando 1 (1), individual aircraft 'H', of I. *Gruppe* (1), 2. *Staffel* (2).

8
Ju 52/3mg3e 22•73 *PEDRO 3* of 3.K/88, *Legion Condor*, Spain, 1937

This aircraft of the '*PEDRO Kette*', under Oberleutnant Rudolf Freiherr von Moreau, displays the pre-war RLM 63 hellgrau/61 dunkelbraun/62 grün splinter pattern, which extends to the engine cowlings. Only the wheel spats remain black. The '22' in the fuselage code denotes a Ju 52/3m, with the '73' being the aircraft number. The name *PEDRO 3* was applied in bold white characters beneath the cockpit, and the rudder was adorned with the Nationalist recognition marking of a black cross over white.

9
Ju 52/3mg3e 22•61 *MARIA DE LA O'* of 3. *Escuadrilla* 'Tres Marias', *Grupo de Bombardeo Nocturno* 2-E-22, Spain, 1937

The Spanish-operated Ju 52/3ms of the Nationalist 3. *Escuadrilla* 2-E-22 retained their original German splinter patterns, but the black fuselage discs were overlaid with a white Nationalist cross marking. The name of the aircraft appeared in bold white characters on the tailplane.

10
Ju 52/3mg3e 22•90 of 2.K/88, *Legion Condor*, possibly Sabadell, Spain, 1937-38

This Junkers of the *Legion Condor* was finished in the standard pre-war RLM 63 hellgrau/61 dunkelbraun/62 grün splinter pattern. It carries a large, toned-down Nationalist cross marking on its fueslage in addition to the standard rudder and wing markings. The significance of the small red cross emblem on a white shield beneath the cockpit is unknown – it may have been an emblem used by 7./KG 153, which operated Ju 52/3ms and may have provided the crew for this machine.

11
Ju 52/3mg3e 22•75 of 3.K/88, *Legion Condor*, Seville, Spain, 1939

This aeroplane is finished in a standard RLM 63 hellgrau/ 61 dunkelbraun/62 grün splinter pattern as seen on most Ju 52/3ms of the *Legion Condor*.

12
Ju 52/3mg4e Wk-Nr 2906 G6+BP of 6./KG.z.b.V.2, Poland, September 1939

This transport is finished in an RLM 70 schwarzgrün/71 dunkelgrün /65 hellblau splinter pattern and the aircraft letter 'B' was in red in conformity with the revised four-character code system introduced in the spring of 1939. This 6. *Staffel* machine had its *Werknummer* applied to the top of its tail fin. Three of the code letters had been lightly daubed with black paint, while the aircraft letter was in red. The positioning of the *Hakenkreuz* indicates an aircraft that had commenced service possibly in 1937 or 1938. It had a supplementary MG 15 fitted to the cockpit canopy.

13
Ju 52/3mg4e(S) Wk-Nr 1348 WL+AFOE, Poland, September 1939

Finished in white with black engine cowlings, this Ju 52/3m ambulance aircraft carries the 'WL' (for '*Wehrmacht Luft*') prefix to its fuselage code to denote a second-line machine. The smaller fuselage *Balkenkreuz* is supplemented by a larger red cross, and the rest of the original five-letter code. Red crosses have also been applied to the roof and wing undersurfaces so as to emphasise the aeroplane's non-combatant role. The tail *Hakenkreuz* is outlined in black and rests over the tail and rudder join.

14
Ju 52/3mg4e G6+JP of 6./KG.z.b.V.2, Poland, September 1939

This Ju 52/3m is camouflaged in a very dusty, low contrast RLM 70 schwarzgrün/71 dunkelgrün /65 hellblau splinter pattern. Its individual aircraft letter 'J' is in a muted red and a *Gruppe* emblem, believed to be a white crow in flight, has been applied to the nose.

15
Ju 52/3mg4e 1Z+GW of 12./KG.z.b.V.1, Poland, September 1939

The individual aircraft letter 'G' on this Ju 52/3m appears to be in black to match the rest of the code. The emblem of 12. *Staffel* of KG.z.b.V.1 adorns the nose and portrays the dancing bear, as seen on the coat of arms of the city of Berlin, against a blue shield topped by a red crown.

16
Ju 52/3mg4e Wk-Nr 6821 VB+UP of KGr.z.b.V.102, Norway, April 1940

This Junkers transport still bears its four-letter code which appears indistinct against the RLM 70 schwarzgrün/71 dunkelgrün /65 hellblau splinter pattern. The new style of *Balkenkreuz*, with thicker white borders, has been applied. The *Werknummer* of the aircraft appears at the top of both the vertical tail surface and the rudder.

17
Ju 52/3mg4e 1Z+LM of 4./KG.z.b.V.1, Norway, April 1940

The remains of a pre-war RLM 63 hellgrau/61 dunkelbraun/62 grün scheme lie beneath a partially applied 70 schwarzgrün/71 dunkelgrün /65 hellblau splinter pattern on this aircraft, which also shows scratch marks and wear and tear along the roof and central fuselage. The wing engines remain in black, as do the undersides of the aircraft for night operations. The white knight chess piece emblem of I./KG.z.b.V.1 is visible on the nose and the aircraft's letter 'L' is in the blue of 4. *Staffel*.

18
Ju 52/3mg4e 1Z+BN of 5./KG.z.b.V.1, Germany, April 1940

This aircraft appears as it was seen while awaiting operations over Scandinavia. It was finished in a 70 schwarzgrün/71 dunkelgrün /65 hellblau scheme and its individual letter was in white.

19
Ju 52/3mg4e 'J' of *Stab*/KG.z.b.V.108, Norway, April 1940

This Ju 52/3m carries only its aircraft letter – 'J' – on the fuselage, probably in red. The winged oil drum emblem of the *Gruppe* is on the nose just ahead of the cockpit. The aircraft's undersides (including the engine cowlings) appear to have been painted black for night flights.

20
Ju 52/3mg4e(S) D-AKLO of *Sanitätsflugbereitschaft* 11, Uetersen, Germany, 1940

With the exception of the nose, engine cowlings and centre areas of the upper wing surfaces, this ambulance aircraft has been painted overall white. The code remains in the five-character civil format, with a red cross applied forward of it. The aircraft was photographed in this finish in 1940 while engaged in ferrying wounded personnel from Scandinavia, but it retained the earlier style tail *Hakenkreuz* on a red tail band.

21
Ju 52/3mg4e T6+MH of 1./*Sturzkampfgeschwader* 2 'Immelmann', Germany, April 1940

This Ju 52/3m probably served as a general transport for the Ju 87-equipped St.G 2. It was finished in the standard 70/71/65 splinter pattern and its individual code letter 'H' was applied in the 1. *Staffel* colour of white. This letter was also applied to the upper surfaces of both wings close to the wingtip. The white edges of the large wing *Balkenkreuze* had been daubed with black paint to tone them down. The aircraft also had a red or blue disc on its nose, at least on its left side, the purpose of which is not known, but it may have been to mask a previous unit emblem or used as an exercise or formation identification marking.

22
Ju 52/3mg4e Wk-Nr 6950 9P+EL of 3./KGr.z.b.V.9, Scandinavia, 1940

This aircraft is something of an anomaly, as its unit code of '9V' indicates a machine of KGr.z.b.V.9 but the leaping stag emblem is known to have been used by aircraft of KGr.z.b.V.106 and KG.z.b.V.172. The aircraft letter 'E' was probably in white, and a short white band ran from the base of the *Balkenkreuz* to the lower edge of the fuselage. The aircraft appears to be finished in an overall coat of RLM 70 or 71, but the fuselage side aft of the door bears some mottling.

23
Ju 52/3mg4e(S) Wk-Nr 6660 D-TABX of *Sanitätsflugbereitschaft* 3, France, 1941

Originally a DLH aircraft, the civil-coded D-TABX saw service as an ambulance machine with the Luftwaffe in the West shortly after the unit's formation. Finished in white, except for its black engine nacelles, the aeroplane had its code applied to its fuselage sides and across its upper wing surfaces. The vertical tail surface carried the State Service Flag formed of a *Hakenkreuz* on a white disc superimposed on a red band across the fin and rudder. At the forward top corner was a white stylised Luftwaffe eagle.

24
Ju 52/3mg4e 5K+VN of II./KG 3, Antwerp-Duerne or Bremen, 1940

Used as a transport for 5./KG 3 at the time of the campaigns in the West, this aircraft was painted in a standard splinter scheme. It had two fuselage bands, probably in white, which had been used as recognition markings by a previous unit and which had been lightly painted over, applied forward of the early style *Balkenkreuz*. The unit code of '5K' was added over two areas of untouched white paint. The individual letter 'V' was in the white of 1. *Staffel*. The *Hakenkreuz* was positioned over the tail fin and rudder join.

25
Ju 52/3mg4e 25+D38 of III./KG.z.b.V.1, possibly Stendal, spring 1940

This aircraft was used for jump-training for German paratroops ahead of operations in Scandinavia and the West. It retained its very faded pre-war RLM 63 hellgrau/61 dunkelbraun/62 grün splinter camouflage, with black engine cowlings and an early-style, weathered red tail band with a *Hakenkreuz* on a white disc.

26
Ju 52/3mg4e 'A' of II./KG.z.b.V.1, the Balkans, April 1941

Finished in the standard 70 schwarzgrün/71 dunkelgrün /65 hellblau splinter pattern, the only identification markings on this aircraft were its white individual code letter and the emblem of II./KG.z.b.V.1 depicting the ancient red eagle of Brandenburg, with each talon clutching a sword, on a white shield. The wing engine nacelles were painted in the theatre colour of yellow.

27
Ju 52/3mg4e 1Z+AZ of IV./KG.z.b.V.1, the Balkans, April 1941

The Balkan theatre identification colour of yellow has been applied to the central engine ring and, in a crudely brushed manner, to the rudder of this aircraft of 15. *Staffel*, KG.z.b.V.1. The aeroplane letter 'A' is also in the *Staffel* colour of yellow, and the emblem of IV. *Gruppe* – a devil figure astride a bomb and carrying a trident – adorns the nose.

28
Ju 52/3mg4e 1Z+HN of II./KG.z.b.V.1, the Balkans, April 1941

Bearing rudder codes that would become more commonplace on Ju 52/3ms as the war progressed, this aircraft was used as a transporter in Greece in April 1941. The '5' denotes 5. *Staffel* and the '8' means it is the eighth aircraft in the unit, and this corresponds to the 'H' in the code, which was in the *Staffel* colour of white. A rear fuselage band was in the theatre recognition colour of yellow, as were the single horizontal stripes on the side of the engine nacelles.

29
Ju 52/3mg4e G6+DX of KGr.z.b.V.105, Greece, May 1941

This dusty Ju 52/3m was finished in a 70 /71/65 splinter pattern, with the first two and fourth letters of the code in weathered and muted black, while the aircraft letter 'D' was in a much stronger colour, probably white. The rudder had been given a wash of yellow, as had, most probably, the engine cowlings.

30
Ju 52/3mg4e of *Sonderkommando Junck*, Mosul, Iraq, May 1941

This aircraft may be a machine of the *Sonderkommando/ KGr.z.b.V.106*, also known as '*Lufttransportstaffel Rother*', intended to provide supplies for the anti-British uprising in Iraq in May 1941. The aeroplane retains a worn standard splinter pattern, as well as German yellow Balkan Theatre markings on its nose and engine cowlings, but the *Balkenkreuze* have been replaced by Iraqi markings, as well as the rudder, which carries the green/white/red/ black national colours of Iraq.

SOURCES AND BIBLIOGRAPHY

MISCELLANEOUS

VIII Fliegerkorps, *Wir Kämpften auf dem Balkan*, (ed.) Hauptmann W Freiherr v. Heintze im Auftrage des VIII.Fliegerkorps, Dresden, 1941

Bundesarchiv-Militärarchiv Freiburg, RL2 series, IV/3, IV/6, IV/7, IV/11. RL7/463. RL 8 series 55, 190, 238

Corum, James S, *The Luftwaffe's Campaigns in Poland and the West 1939-1940: A Case Study of Handling Innovation in Wartime*, Security and Defence Quarterly, National Defence University, Warsaw, 2103

Förderverein Technikmuseum 'Hugo Junkers' Dessau E V, *Junkers – Pioneer of Aviation*, Dessau-Roßlau, undated (available at www.technikmuseum-dessau.de)

Hagedorn, Dan, *The Chaco War 1928-1935*. Download text for *Latin American Air Wars and Aircraft 1912-1969*, Hikoki Publications, Crowborough, 2006

UK National Archives, AIR20/7700, 7702, 7703, 7708, 7709. Also misc. files in AIR26, AIR40, HW1 and WO208

De Zeng IV, Henry L and Stankey, Douglas J, *Luftwaffe Officer Career Summaries*, Version: April 2015

Zindel, Ernst, *Die Geschichte und Entwicklung des Junkers-Flugzeugbaus von 1910 bis 1945 und bis zum endgültigen Ende 1970*, Deutsche Gesellschaft für Luft- und Raumfahrt, Köln, 1979

WEBSITES

Mulder, Rob, *Air Cargo a la Junkers: Air Express Co Ltd, Luftfrako and Deutramp*
- *Airline companies in Rumania (1918-1945)*
- *AB Aerotransport and the Junkers G 24*
all at www.europeanairlines.no

Axis History and *Axis History Forum* at www.axishistory.com

Golden Years of Aviation (German Registers) at http://www.airhistory.org.uk/gy/home.html

Hugo Junkers – Ein Leben für die Technik at www.junkers.de

The Battle for Stalingrad at www.stalingrad.net

The Chaco War (1932-1935), ICRC Resource Centre at http://www.icrc.org/eng/resources/documents/misc/5gkebj.htm#

The history of BMW aero engines at www.bmwgroup.com

The *Hugo Junkers Homepage* at http://hugojunkers.pytalhost.com/ju_home.htm

The Luftwaffe 1933-1945 at www.w2.dk

Falke Eins – The Luftwaffe Blog at falkeeins.blogspot.co.uk

LEMB Stammkennzeichen Database Project at http://www.luftwaffe-experten.org/stammkennzeichen.html

Hermansson, Bengt, *Flykten till Bonarpshed* at www.forcedlandingcollection.se

Hugo Junkers: A short biography and his technical achievement, www.technikmuseum-dessau.de

SELECTED PUBLISHED BOOKS

Budraß, Lutz, *Flugzeugindustrie und Luftrüstung in Deutschland 1918-1945*, Droste Verlag, Düsseldorf, 1998

Claasen, Adam R A, *Hitler's Northern War – The Luftwaffe's Ill-Fated Campaign, 1940-1945*, University Press of Kansas, Lawrence, 2001

Cornwell, Peter D, *The Battle of France Then and Now*, Battle of Britain International, Harlow, 2007

Dinter, Horst, *Meine Erlebnisse als Ju 52-Transportflieger 1940-1944*, Stedinger Verlag, Lemwerder, 2004

Drum, General der Flieger Karl, *The German Air Force in the Spanish Civil War (Condor Legion)*, USAF Historical Studies: No 150, MA/AH Publishing – Sunflower University Press, Manhattan, undated

Erfurth, Helmut, *Zivile Luftfahrt im dritten Reich: Glanz und Elend des deutschen Luftverhrs 1933-1945*, GeraMond, München, 2005

Fischer von Poturzyn, Hptm. A D Friedrich Andreas, *Junkers und die Weltluftfahrt*, Richard Pflaum Verlag, München, 1935

Fleischer, Wolfgang, *German Air-Dropped Weapons to 1945*, Midland Publishing, Hinckley, 2004

Forsyth, Robert, *Junkers Ju 52 – A History: 1930-1945*, Classic Publications, Manchester, 2014

Hagedorn, Dan, *Latin American Air Wars and Aircraft 1912-1969*, Hikoki Publications, Crowborough, 2006

Homze, Edward L, *Arming the Luftwaffe*, University of Nebraska Press, Lincoln, 1996

Hooton, E R, *Phoenix Triumphant – The Rise and Rise of the Luftwaffe*, Arms and Armour Press, London, 1994

Hoppe, Henry, *Junkers Ju 52/3m – The German World War II Frontline Veteran/Der Luftwaffe-Veteran an allen Fronten*, AirDoc, Erlangen, 2004

Howson, Gerald, *Aircraft of the Spanish Civil War 1936-1939*, Putnam, London, 1990

Irving, David, *The Rise and Fall of the Luftwaffe – The Life of Erhard Milch*, Weidenfeld and Nicolson, London, 1973

Kay, Antony L, *Junkers Aircraft & Engines 1913-1945*, Putnam Aeronautical Books, London, 2004

Kössler, Karl, *Transporter – wer kennt sie schon! Die Kennzeichen der Transportfliegerverbände der Luftwaffe von 1937-1945*, Alba Buchverlag, Düsseldorf, 1976

Lange, Bruno, *Tante Ju – Alles über die Ju 52*, Verlag Dieter Hoffmann, Mainz, 1976

Maier, Klaus A, *Guernica 26.4.1937: Die deutsche intervention in Spanien und der 'Fall Guernica'*, Rombach and Co., Freiburg, 1975

Morgenstern, Karl, and Plath, Dietmar, *Eurasia Aviation Corporation: Junkers & Lufthansa in China 1931-1943*, GeraMond Verlag, München, 2006

Morzik, Generalmajor A D Fritz, *German Air Force Airlift Operations*, USAF Historical Division, Arno Press, New York, 1961

Morzik, Fritz and Hümmelchen, Gerhard, *Die deutschen Transportflieger im Zweiten Weltkrieg,* Bernard & Graefe Verlag, Frankfurt am Main, 1966

Playfair, Maj-Gen I S O (et al.), *The Mediterranean and Middle East Volume 1*, HMSO, London, 1954

Pegg, Martin, *Transporter: Volume One – Luftwaffe Transport Units 1939-1943*, Classic Publications, Hersham, 2006

Proctor, Raymond L, *Hitler's Luftwaffe in the Spanish Civil War*, Greenwood Press, Westport, 1983

Ries, Karl, *Luftwaffe Band 1 – Die Maulwürfe (Geheimer Aufbau 1919-1935) Vol.1, The Moles (Underground Activity 1919-1935)*, Verlag Dieter Hoffmann, Mainz, 1970

Ries, Karl, *Luftwaffen Story 1935-1939*, Verlag Dieter Hoffmann, Mainz, 1974

Ries, Karl and Ring, Hans, *The Legion Condor – A History of the Luftwaffe in the Spanish Civil War 1936-1939*, Schiffer Military History, West Chester, 1992

Schlaug, Georg, *Die deutschen Lastensegler-Verbände 1937-1945 – Eine Chronik aus Berichten, Tagebüchern, Dokumenten*, Motorbuch Verlag, Stuttgart, 1985

Stapfer, Hans-Heiri, Mau, Hans-Joachim and Punka, George, *Junkers Ju 52 in action*, Squadron/Signal publications, Carrollton, 2002

Suchenwirth, Richard, *The Development of the German Air Force 1919-1939*, Arno Press, New York, June 1968

Supf, Peter, *Das Buch der deutschen Fluggeschichte: Band 2*, Drei Brunnen Verlag, Stuttgart, 1958

Völker, Karl-Heinz, *Die Entwicklung der Militärischen Luftfahrt in Deutschland 1920-1933*, Deutsche Verlags-Anstalt, Stuttgart, 1962

Völker, Karl-Heinz, *Die Deutsche Luftwaffe 1933-1939 – Aufbau, Führung und Rüstung der Luftwaffe sowie die Entwicklung der deutschen Luftkriegstheorie*, Deutsche Verlags-Anstalt, Stuttgart, 1967

Wagner, Wolfgang, *Hugo Junkers: Pionier der Luftfahrt*, Bernard and Graefe Verlag, Bonn, 1996

De Zeng IV, Henry L, and Stankey, Douglas G, *Bomber Units of the Luftwaffe 1933-1945 – A Reference Source, Volume 2*, Classic Publications, Hersham, 2008

INDEX

Note: locators in **bold** refer to illustrations and captions.

1./Sturzkampfgeschwader 2: **21** (**43**, 92–93)
1ª Escuadrilla 27, 28, 30–31
2-G-22: **49**, 51
2ª Escuadrilla 28, 30–31
3ª Escuadrilla **28**, 30–31
4ª Escuadrilla 30–31

A/88 reconnaissance and maritime reconnaissance Gruppen 29, 50

Balkans (1941) **26** (**45**, 93), **27** (**46**, 93), **28** (**46**, 93), **29** (**47**, 93), **80**, 80–89, **81**, **83**, **85**, **87**
Bombengeschwader (BG) 1: 22, 23

Chaco War (1932-35) 14–16, **15**

DFS 230 assault gliders 68, 69, 70–71, 88
Dornier Do 11 aircraft 22, 23
Dornier Do 17 aircraft 49
Dornier Do 23 aircraft 24

E-22: 31, **9** (**37,** 92)
Escuadra B 28, 30

F 13 airliners 7, 9
France (1940-41) **23** (**44**, 93), 67–79, **75**, **76**
Franco, General Francisco 25, 27, 28

G 24 transport aircraft 8, **9**
Göring, Hermann 21, 25, 29, 60
Grosse Kampffliegerschule **4** (**34**, 91)
Grupo de Bombardeo Nocturno 30–31, **9** (**37**, 92), **49**, 51

Heinkel He 51 aircraft 26, 28, 30, 48–49, 50
Heinkel He 70 aircraft **52**
Heinkel He 111 aircraft 51, 56–57, 68, 72, 89
Heinkel He III B-1 aircraft 49
Henke, Flugkapitän Alfred 25–26, 27, 28
Hitler, Adolf 25, 26, 27, 28, 56, 61, 65, 80, 81, 89

Iraq (1941) **30** (**47**, 93), 89, **89**

J/88 fighter Gruppe 29, 50
Junkers, Professor Hugo 6, 7, **7**, **8**, 9–10, 13, 17, 21–22, **22**
Junkers, Klaus 19, 24
Junkers J 23 (G 23) transport aircraft 8
Junkers J 31 (G 31) transport aircraft 9, 18
Junkers Ju 52/3m aircraft **16**, **33–47**, 91–93
　armament 22–23, **23**, 24, **28**, 48, **56**, **57**, **60**
　cockpit 19, **56**
　design and development 10–14, **11**, **12**, 17–20, 23–24
　engines 11–12, 13, 14, **18**, 19
　fuselage 10, **11**, 15, **73**
　markings **6,** 15, **18**, **20**, **21**, 29, **30**, **51**, **55**, **57**, **58**, **64**, **66**, 68, **79**, **83**, **89**
　paint finishes 15, **17**, **53**, **79**, **80**, **83**

propellers 13–14
variants **7**, 90
wings 10–11, 13, 14, **18**
Junkers Ju 86 aircraft 49, **54**
Junkers Ju 87 aircraft 73, 88
Junkers Ju 90 aircraft 89

K/88 bomber Gruppe 29, **29**, 31, **48**, 49, 50, 51
　2.K/88: **10** (**37**, 92)
　3.K/88: **8** (**36**, 91), **11** (**38**, 92)
KG 3: **24** (**44**, 93)
KG 152: **54**
　2./KG 152: **7** (**36**, 91)
　7./KG 152 78
　II./KG 152: **54**
　III./KG 152: 24
　IV./KG 152: 52
KG 153:
　7./KG 153: **21**
　I./KG 153: 24, **52**
　II./KG 153: 24
　III./KG 153: 24
　IV./KG 153: 25
KG 154: 24
KG 155:
　II./KG 155: 24
　III./KG 155: 24
KG 253 24
KG 254: **5** (**35**, 91)
　I./KG 254: 24–25
KG 753: **3** (**34**, 91)
KGr.z.b.V.1: **6** (**35**, 91), 52, 78
KGr.z.b.V.2: 52, 62
KGr.z.b.V.5: 68
KGr.z.b.V.9: 53, 55, 68, 74–76, 77
　1./KGr.z.b.V.9: 74–75
　2./KGr.z.b.V.9: 75
　3./KGr.z.b.V.9: **22** (**43**, 93), 75
　4./KGr.z.b.V.9: 75–76
KGr.z.b.V.11: 68, 77
KGr.z.b.V.12: 68, 79
　I./KGr.z.b.V.12: 77
KGR.z.b.V.40: 82
KGr.z.b.V.60: 82, 86
KGr.z.b.V.101: 62, 84
KGr.z.b.V.102: **16** (**40**, 92), 62, 64, **65**, 66, 84, 86
KGr.z.b.V.103: 62, 63, 64, 66
KGr.z.b.V.104: 62, 82
KGr.z.b.V.105: **29** (**47**, 93), 62, 82
KGr.z.b.V.106: 62, 66, 78
　3./KGr.z.b.V.106: 78
KGr.z.b.V.107: 62, 64, 78
KGr.z.b.V.108: **19** (**42**, 92), 62, 64, 78
KGr.z.b.V.172: 84
　1./KGr.z.b.V.172: 68, 76–77
KGr.z.b.V.900: 783
KG.z.b.V.1: 53, 61–62, 68, 72–73, 78, 83
　4./KG.z.b.V.1: **17** (**41**, 92)
　5./KG.z.b.V.1: **18** (**41**, 92)
　7./KG.z.b.V.1: 63
　12./KG.z.b.V.1: **15** (**40**, 92)
　I./KG.z.b.V.1: 77, 84, 86

II./KG.z.b.V.1: **26** (**45**, 93), **28** (**46**, 93), 62, 65, 77, 84
III./KG.z.b.V.1: **25** (**45**, 93), **55**, 68, 71, 81–82
IV./KG.z.b.V.1: **27** (**46**, 93), 77
KG.z.b.V.2: **56,** 62, 68, 78, 79, 83, 84, 86
　6./KG.z.b.V.2: **12** (**38**, 92), **14** (**39**, 92)
　I./KG.z.b.V.2: 79, 86
　II./KG.z.b.V.2: 86
　IV./KG.z.b.V.2: 54, 57, 58
KG.z.b.V.172: 52–53
　I./KG.z.b.V.172: 73
Krause, Hauptmann Rudolf 77, 84

Legion Condor **26**, 29–52, **10** (**37**, 92), **11** (**38**, 92), **51**
'Leticia Incident,' the 16

Messerschmitt Bf 109 aircraft 50
Messerschmitt Bf 110 aircraft 63, 89
MG 15 machine guns **23**, 24, **28**, **57**, **60**
Milch, Erich 13, 17–18, 19, 21–22, 28–29
Morzik, Oberstleutnant Friedrich-Wilhelm 52, 68, 72–73, 83

Netherlands (1940) 67–79, **75**
Norway (1940) **16** (**40**, 92), **17** (**41**, 92), **19** (**42**, 92), 61–66, **62**, **64**, **65**

Poland (1939) **12** (**38**, 92), **13** (**39**, 92), **14** (**39**, 92), **15** (**40**, 92), 53–58, **55**, **56**, **57**, **58**

Regierungsstaffel **17**, **2** (**33**, 91)
Richthofen, Generalmajor Wolfram Frhr. von 32, 50, 54–55, 56–58, 88

Sanitätsflugbereitschaft 3: **23** (**44**, 93)
Sanitätsflugbereitschaft 11: **20** (**42**, 92)
Sonderkommando Junck **30** (**47**, 93)
Spanish Civil War (1936-39) 25–51, **8** (**36**, 91), **9** (**37**, 92), **10** (**37**, 92), **11** (**38**, 92)

Treaty of Versailles (1919) 6, 8, **8**
Tripartite pact (1941) 80

VB/88 Gruppe 50

Winter War (1939-40) **16** (**40**, 92), **17** (**41**, 92), **19** (**42**, 92), **22** (**43**, 93), 61–66, **62**, **64**, **65**
World War II (1939-45) 53–89, **62**
　Balkans (1941) **26** (**45**, 93), **27** (**46**, 93), **28** (**46**, 93), **29** (**47**, 93), **80**, 80–89, **81**, **83**, **85**, **87**
　France (1941) **23** (**44**, 93)
　Iraq (1941) **30** (**47**, 93), 89, **89**
　Operation Fall Gelb (1940) 67–79, **75**, **76**
　Poland (1939) **12** (**38**, 92), **13** (**39**, 92), **14** (**39**, 92), **15** (**40**, 92), 53–58, **55**, **56**, **57**, **58**
　Winter War (1939-40) **16** (**40**, 92), **17** (**41**, 92), **19** (**42**, 92), 61–66, **64**, **65**

Ziervogel, Major Dr. Max 62, 78
Zindel, Ernst 6, **7**, 10, 11, 13–14, 23–24, 58